# ALL SHERMAN IS LOOKING TO YOUR SUCCESS:

## THE 1898 - 1899 LETTERS OF
## THE ROBERTS FAMILY OF SHERMAN, TEXAS
## AND
## STANLY ROBERTS AT PRINCETON UNIVERSITY

Edited by **Heather Palmer**

ALL SHERMAN IS LOOKING TO YOUR SUCCESS:

THE 1898 - 1899 LETTERS OF

THE ROBERTS FAMILY OF SHERMAN, TEXAS

AND

STANLY ROBERTS AT PRINCETON UNIVERSITY

Edited by **Heather Palmer**

The Sherman Preservation League Press
Sherman, Texas

This volume, its editing and presentation
© 2004 Heather Ruth Palmer
All Rights Reserved

Letter texts © Phyllis Roberts

With the exclusion of no more than 200 words for use in a review, neither this book nor any portion of it may be copied or reproduced in any way without prior written permission from the publisher

Published by
The Sherman Preservation League Press
P. O. Box 159
Sherman, Texas 75091-0159

ISBN 0-9760489-0-6

1. Palmer, Heather -- Editor
2. Roberts Family -- Letters
3. United States -- History -- Personal Letters
4. United States -- History -- Nineteenth Century
5. Texas History -- Nineteenth Century

Dedicated to my husband,
Dr. Mark Alan Riedesel
Princeton Class of 1977
   -- Heather Palmer


Dedicated to the memory of my husband, Stanly's youngest son, Professor Emeritus, University of Texas at Austin,
Dr. Royston Murphy Roberts
   -- Phyllis Roberts


Special Appreciation to
Judith Roberts Bryant,
daughter of Stanly's oldest son,
Stanly Roberts, Jr.,
For her valuable help.

And to David and Mignon Plyler
For their support of
The Sherman Preservation League Press

   -- Heather Palmer & Phyllis Roberts

Stanly's parents rarely posed for pictures. This memento of an outing made by C.N. and Emma Roberts with the Murphy family was taken around 1907 at the time of the marriage of their children, Stanly and Leska.

Two photographs of Stanly Roberts taken while he was a student at Princeton University, school year 1898-1899. His face had been badly injured while looking at equipment at a construction site when a child.

C. N. Roberts in a 1906 picture of the Robert's family home. The 1896 Eastlake home in Sherman, Texas was built for under $9,000. Today the historic house museum still retains almost all of its original features, including the gas and electric chandeliers, numerous "art glass" windows, massive pocket doors and extensive built-in woodwork.

Kirtley Darnall, the woman who lived with her mother and sister across the street from the Roberts family until 1899. She was so much Emma's choice of a wife for her son that Emma always kept Kirtley's picture in her room -- even after Stanly married another girl in the neighborhood.

The engaging and vivacious Leska Murphy, taken with her parrot at about the time when Stanly was a student at Princeton. As she had one brown eye and one blue eye she delighted in singing the popular song, "Will Ye Marry a Brown Eyed or a Blue Eyed Girl" and informing the men who courted her that with her they would not have to choose. Stanly's and Leska's romance blossomed not during his college days but during hers six years later.

**INTRODUCTION**

The relationship between Captain Charles Nathan Roberts and his only surviving child, Charles Stanly Roberts, was particularly close. For most of his young life "Stanly" had been groomed by "C.N." to join the family's successful wholesale hardware business in Sherman, Texas upon Stanly's graduation from college. C.N. knew first hand that once his son had begun full-time employment with the firm Stanly would have little time for travel or leisure. To give one last year of youth to his beloved son, C.N. arranged that after Stanly was graduated from Austin College in Texas in May of 1898, Stanly would re-do his Senior year at Princeton University, gaining another year of education along with the opportunity to tour the East Coast.

From the 1070's until the first World War it was not uncommon for young men such as Stanly, with a newly completed degree from a small college in the West, to retake a Senior year at a prestigious Eastern university. It was probably the strong religious ties between Princeton and her own minister which caused Stanly's mother, Emma Ethel Royston Roberts, to whole-heartedly support the plan to send Stanly to Princeton for a year. Stanly became one of eight young men who entered Princeton's Senior Class, 192 of whom would receive diplomas in 1899.

Armed with liberal spending money and a lengthy list of the names of his parents' East Coast relatives and church friends, Stanly left home in Sherman for Princeton in September, 1898. Although some of Stanly's letters are missing, having been remailed at the time to far-flung relatives, most of the letters which passed between Stanly and his parents were later collected together and kept by Stanly's mother, Emma. The letters are still in the possession of the family and it is through the gracious generosity of Phyllis Roberts, Stanly's daughter-in-law, that they are being published.

The letters capture the spirit of the late nineteenth century with unusual clarity; the details of travel, study, and the daily life of the era are fresh and vivid. The distance of time from the years of the letters to our own year is lessened by the immediacy inherent in the words, and a reader of the letters gains a clear picture of life over one hundred years ago.

The letters also tell a more focused story of one community, one university and one family. Residents of Sherman, Texas will find in the letters a rare glimpse of their town. Graduates of Princeton will enjoy the tales of college life. All readers will enjoy the family portrait which is depicted in the open and caring letters. C.N. and Emma had a friendly and loving marriage and their joy in each other and their faith had sustained them so completely in their many tragedies that these letters show no hint of all the sorrows they had suffered.

C.N.'s marriage to Emma was his second. His first wife, Mary English, had died giving birth to a son who had also died. Even earlier in his life he had experienced sorrow when his family had divided loyalties during

## Introduction

the Civil War; C.N. was with the Confederacy as a Commissary Officer while some of his brothers fought with the Federal Army. C.N. had also known the sorrows of business failures before gaining success and, with Emma, he had grieved at the deaths of several children.

The deaths of two children were only the final installments in a life of loss for Emma. Both of her parents had died before she was ten and after a youth of being passed from relative to relative she had only recently been reunited with both of her beloved sisters when they too had died. At about the same time her first two children died, Emma also had to mourn the loss of the little nephew she had reared. Even Stanly had almost been lost to her in childhood when he was badly injured at a construction site.

By 1898, however, the sorrows of C.N.'s and Emma's pasts were being diluted by a joyful present. C.N.'s business was thriving and the family had just moved into a magnificent Eastlake mansion which had been built to their specifications. With just the help of Charlie, a day servant who did yard work and some cooking, Emma ran her home and actively participated in numerous charity and cultural groups. Crockett Street, where they lived, was one of the two long residential streets for the more wealthy citizens of Sherman, the county seat of Grayson County, Texas. Their street was served by a trolley line and C.N. could "commute" the dozen blocks to his business in just a few minutes.

The large city block around their house was filled with the products of Emma's "green thumb" and, as these letters show, would come to be dominated by a gazebo, sited on the foundation of their first house in Sherman. The elegant but comfortable new house, built in 1896, was serviced by both gas and electricity and had numerous fireplaces, stained glass "art" windows, and Eastlake-style woodwork details. Although there were two bathrooms outfitted with beautiful tubs and sinks, Emma had resisted the modern innovation of "an outhouse indoors" and there were no indoor toilets until 1907.

The downstairs rooms held a wonderful piano (a wedding gift from C.N. to Emma) and rich furnishings. Numerous works of history and literature filled many shelves, but the couple's favorite reading matter was religious. C.N. & Emma were devout Presbyterians and the tenets of their church guided every aspect of their lives. They were kind, generous, and earnest in their faith. Emma eschewed colors in dress and wore no jewelry and both Emma and C.N. were strongly opposed to alcohol and cards, but this sternness for themselves was rarely inflicted on anyone else. Beneath her somber exterior Emma was always a woman with a keen sense of humor. Under the sober exterior of a prominent and pious businessman C.N. was enough a man of the world to give greater leeway to his son than the standards to which he held himself.

At twenty-one Stanly was all that a fond parent could wish. His manners were engaging and open and he had the same love of life as had his parents. If he were not as much of a scholar as was his mother, Stanly did already possess the keen business sense praised by his father. The friendliness and candor which permeate both sides of the correspondence is not the least of the letters' appeal.

While it was not uncommon for college boys one hundred years ago to write home at least once a week, as Stanly did, Stanly had a special reason, beyond that of affection, for keeping closely in touch with his parents. Later letters and family

*Introduction*                                                        5

recollections indicate that Stanly was lonely at Princeton. For Stanly, who had been the leader of many campus activities at Austin College and who was extremely popular in his town and church, that was quite a change.

    Before Stanly's arrival for a Senior year at Princeton, most of the other members of his class had been together at the college for several years; many of them had also known each other previously at preparatory schools. It is therefore not surprising that Stanly's recollections of life at Princeton revealed that while he was a student there he felt somewhat outside the circle of camaraderie. His relations with the other members of the Senior Class were cordial, but he formed no life-long friendships with any of the boys in his class. In the sweet letter he wrote for inclusion in his ten year reunion book Stanly "covered" the fact that he could not comment on recent interactions with any members of his class by writing, "We are so far from Headquarters down here in Texas." Those who know of the exemplary life of service which Stanly lived can only hope the great affection always felt for him by his family, employees and town members negated any sting he may have felt when his lack of friends in his Princeton class was underscored by the fact his letter appeared under a banner which gave his name incorrectly.

    As Stanly was one of only a very few boys who lived off campus he was further handicapped in his endeavors to make friends. While most of the Senior class lived in luxurious dormitory rooms which boasted stone fireplaces, leaded glass windows and fine furnishings, Stanly lived in a small old boarding house. No other college students lived near him. As Stanly's parents could easily have paid the on campus housing rate of between $3. to $7. a week it must be supposed that the problem was that Stanly had joined the class after dormitory space had been assigned and the boarding house was his only viable option.

Besides his late inclusion in the class and his off campus living, another factor which may have contributed to Stanly's inability to leap into friendships at Princeton was the strained mood on the campus the year he was there. It was just a few years later, in 1902, that Woodrow Wilson was unanimously elected President of the college, partly in reaction to the general disgust felt at the way the previous genial President of the college had failed to control hazing and boisterous high spirits. The mood on campus during the school year Stanly was at Princeton is part of the history of the college told by Samuel A. Schreiner in his engaging work, <u>A Place Called Princeton</u>, published by Arbor House in 1984. As Schreiner relates, Wilson later compared student life at the Campus before his presidency as a sideshow livelier than the main tent.

At graduation 111 of the boys in Stanly's class admitted to having participated in hazing. Stories told in later years of the hazing process reveal a type of behavior which the gentle Stanly would have had a difficult time condoning. One can imagine the incredulity and disgust someone of his sensibilities felt the first weeks on campus when he saw boys he had hoped would become friends participating in activities which he could not endorse. Stanly was not alone in his disgust at the actions of some of his classmates. After all, if 111 of the Seniors were hazers, then about eighty were not. The dissenters, however, were not a cohesive group and their varied backgrounds and, perhaps, implied shyness, kept them from becoming a team.

*Introduction* 7

The class "leaders" were emphatically not shy. While bravado may account for some of the numbers, it is still noteworthy that in a survey at graduation 95 members of Stanly's class claimed they owned their own corkscrew, 119 declared they were card players and, at a school which officially frowned on the practice, 114 claimed they were dancers. Stanly did not drink, play cards, or dance. The jokes recounted in alumni records over the forty years following graduation present a picture of college life which was contrary to many values to which Stanly was accustomed. Stanly was at twenty-one the strongly committed Christian he would remain all of his life. He took all aspects of his Presbyterian faith very seriously and he allowed no room in his mind at all for the prevalent iconoclastic mood on college campuses in the late 1890's. It is a good guess that his predominately East Coast classmates thought of the religious Texas newcomer in their midst as very provincial indeed. In a class where boys nicknamed "Goat" and "Beef" were the social leaders Stanly, a year older, was called "The Kid".

Tensions also arose that year, on Princeton and on other college campuses, from the divided viewpoints about the implications of the Spanish-American war. The impact of the war was strengthened at Princeton by the death of a classmate, Ralph Wilson Simonds, on 5 February 1899 in what the alumni book described as "a skirmish between the American and Philippine forces at Manilla." Some students and professors strenuously opposed any American involvement outside of the contiguous states and territories, while others believed the war and subsequent events were an inevitable and right step in America's "Manifest Destiny." Stanly's favorite Princeton teacher, none other than future United States President Woodrow

Wilson, told an alumni group during Stanly's year at Princeton that like it or not, American colonialism was a reality: "The nation has broken its shell and bids fair to run a momentous career."

Stanly was wise enough to know that he could gain a lot from his year at Princeton, even without becoming a leader with the "in" crowd. His honest genial nature ensured that at the very least his relations with other students were pleasant. He loved to sing and he had a beautiful voice. When, in the Spring, the Seniors gathered outside to sing, Stanly finally felt a part of his class. His integrity and earnestness also must surely have won him the respect of his professors, even if he was not their best student.

Recollections and later family letters indicate that Stanly believed that part of his inability to fit into life at Princeton was not so much his late arrival to the class or his off campus housing or even the differences over hazing and religious practices but that some of his classmates felt Stanly was not up to their social or economic standing. If that were so, then the general class estimation of Stanly must have seemed almost confirmed when they read the one year graduation anniversary handbook for his class. The boys who had been the social leaders in the class still appeared to be leaders in the working world while Stanly, meanwhile, modestly listed his occupation as "Store clerk" in his Father's company.

Things had evened out for them all, however, by their thirtieth reunion and since Stanly may not have been inclined to write it up it is not hard to imagine that it was Stanly's wife who wrote his 1929 listing: "President of Roberts, Stanford & Taylor, Director Woodlawn Country Club, Director Sherman Chamber of Commerce, Director Sherman

## Introduction

Y.M.C.A., Director Merchants & Planters Bank, Member Board of Trustees of Austin College, Chairman of the Board of United Churches of Sherman, Chairman of the Board of Deacons of the First Presbyterian Church."

Although always modest about all areas of his life, Stanly was always proud of his Princeton degree and the fact that he had studied under Woodrow Wilson. In later years he actively participated in the annual fundgiving and he was praised in his alumni obituary. He was one of the last surviving members of his class at his death in 1972.

So that readers can feel the immediacy of the material, the texts of the letters are presented here exactly as they were written. To have presented only the dramatic sections would have been to lose the charm of an era which had so perfected the art of letter writing that much verbiage could be constructed from very little "news". An editorial introduction precedes each letter and the few necessary editorial emendations within a letter are enclosed in brackets.

## THE FIRST LETTER

From Stanly in Philadelphia
16 September 1898

The first surviving letter was actually the second one which Stanly had sent home en route to Princeton. His exuberant description of train travel here foreshadowed the enthusiasm with which Stanly would greet his entire school year. Kirtley, who was mentioned in this letter and in many others, was a young woman who lived on the same street as the Roberts family. She was somewhat older than Stanly and he did not care for her romantically, but Emma had hopes of a romance developing between them. Ever courteous, even if not completely obliging in this matter, Stanly did at least remember to mention passing through the town of Clayton where Kirtley had relatives living.

The letter, written in large bold handwriting, covers the fronts of eight pages of lined letterhead of The Windsor Hotel, 1217-1231 Filbert Street, Philadelphia, PA. It was addressed, like all of Stanly's letters, simply to "Capt. C.N. Roberts, Sherman, Texas".

*Philadelphia, PA*
*Sept 16, 1898*

*Dear Papa:*

*When you see my address at the top of this paper I guess you will begin to wonder where I will turn up next but really I guess the next time I will be in Princeton.*

*To take things as they come I will have to go back to the Terminal Hotel where I left off in my last letter.*

*I went down to see Mr Stevens and he gave me three passes, one to Indianapolis, one from there to Pittsburgh and one from Pittsburgh to Philadelphia. I left St Louis at <u>100</u> P.M. Thursday on the Limited #2[.] The fastest train to New York. I took the New York sleeper and maybe you think it wasnt* [sic] *pretty. It was decidedly the finest sleeper on the line. There were six other Pullmans on our train and it was by far the best. One of the men on it said that he thought it had been fixed up for som[e] exposition or something. I only bought my sleeper ticket through to Pittsburg as the conductor said I would have to change trains there. The Limited east of Pittsburg didn't carry anybody except those who <u>paid</u> full fare. I hated to give up my sleeper and everything there although I suppose I would have gotten another that would* [have] *done as well but I didn't have to give it up after all. The Limited (the one I was on West of Pittsburgh) got into Pittsburgh one hour and twenty minutes late (The engine lost a bolt off the ejector shaft, whatever that may be) and so when we got to Pittsburgh the Limited from there had been gone an hour and our sleeper was put on a slow train and I came clear in to Philadelphia in it.*

## 12   All Sherman is Looking to Your Success

When I say <u>slow</u> train above I mean it stopped at more places than the limited. As to its slowness you can judge for yourself. We had a long train of thirteen coaches. I timed it twice. The first time we made nine miles in nine and seven eights [sic] minutes and the next time 13 miles in 13 3/4 minutes. Not too bad was it. But that isn't anything compared to what we did on The Limited yesterday. We were an hour and twenty minutes late and trying to make it up and it actually made my head ache to look at the ground, it went by so fast.

I use[d] to think down in Texas that if the trains would only go fifty miles an hour I would be satisfied but I found my self complaining several times to day because it took us 62 or 64 minutes to make a mile. [Probably he meant "100 miles".]

There was a wreck on our road yesterday. We passed it this morning. Freight train ran away down the side of the mountain and if it didn't pile things up, it most. Nobody was hurt however.

I got into Philadelphia tonight (Friday) at 7 05 just five minutes too late to catch the last train that stopped at Princeton Junction. Came down here to the Windsor hotel (block and a half from depot) and got a room. It is a big hotel and they only charge me $1.50 for supper and my room and breakfast. I went up to my room washed up a little, came down to supper and then went back to the station to get my ticket for in the morning and get my trunk checked. The man took my check and gave me another, said he couldnt [sic] find my trunk but it was probable that it would not come in until 4 AM tomorrow. I leave at 6 50 in the morning for Princeton and Ill get there a little after eight. When I left the station I went to a barber shop, got a haircut shave and shampoo and maybe you think my head doesn't feel a little cleaner. It ought to be anyway the man squirted the hose on it.

Then, I came back to the hotel to write this letter and here I am. It is five minutes after ten now so I think I'll stop and go to bed. By the way Wanamakers is closed tonight and wont [sic] open till 8 am so Ill have to put off my purchases. I could stay over a while in the morning but I want all day tomorrow to see about my room at Princeton. My ticket to Princeton cost me $1.18.

Goodbye with lots of love to you both

Stanly

P.S.

I didn't see anything of Grace and tell Kirtley all I saw of Clayton was a white looking streak as the train went by. We were way up in the sixties (miles an hour I mean) when we passed there.

Stanly

P.S. #2 If I write many more letters the size of this you'll have to send me some stamps or Ill go "busted"

S-----

## THE SECOND LETTER

From C.N. and Emma in Sherman
21 September 1898

The first surviving joint letter from Emma and C. N. contains charming details of their daily lives and the relations between family members. Although Stanly was not the first young man from Sherman to attend Princeton for a school year it was an unusual enough occurrence to be much talked of in the Roberts' circles. Because Princeton University was known to Texans at that time primarily because its Seminary supplied so many Presbyterian churches, there was a great deal of joking that the merry Stanly would "end up" a minister. Both C.N. and Emma taught Sunday school classes (hence the reference to a "teacher's" meeting) and were close friends with many ministers in the Presbyterian churches in Texas. Both the "Dr. Moore" and "Dr. Taylor" who are mentioned here and in other letters had been instrumental in helping Stanly be accepted at Princeton.

Much of the appeal of this letter comes from the way in which C.N. addressed his collegiate son, almost as though they were already the business partners they would be for the following twenty-five years. The scheme C.N. wrote of in this letter was his hope to involve a number of area businessmen in working together to improve the fledgling textile business in Sherman.

The only direction on the envelop was "Mr. C. S. Roberts, Princeton, N.J."

*Wednesday Sept. 21, 1898*

*Dear Son,*

*You have been gone a week yesterday and it seems like a whole month. We received your letter written from Philadelphia yesterday morning I am sorry you could not do your shopping while there, but think it was best for you to have the whole day at Princeton. The last letter you received was written Saturday, so I will begin with Sunday morning. Charlie was late about breakfast and I was late about getting ready so your papa had to leave me to come later. I caught the* [trolley] *car that Kirtley and Grace took. The latter went on to my class. There were twenty seven Nash girls at S.S.* [Sunday School] *Dr Moore's text was "Woe to them that are at ease in Zion". His text at night was "Who forgiveth all thine iniquities; who healeth all thy diseases". He preached two good sermons, and we had a good singing and good congregations. Prof- McLanchlin heard the review in the afternoon.*

*We had a good Teachers meeting though the weather was very threatening. After Teacher meeting we came home by Judge Galloways. They returned Saturday afternoon, went first to the hotel and engaged two rooms and then went down to the house to get some clothes. They went up stairs and opened up the rooms and then concluded they could not go back to the hotel. So we found them at home.*

They received us in the library Mrs Galloway said she would grieve just as much at the hotel shut up in those rooms would feel like she was in a jail. She said judge seemed happier that night than at any time since Reub's death. They are very sad and desolate. I went over and spent all monday afternoon with Mrs. Galloway. Mrs. Baty was also there and Mrs. Wilson was with her during the morning.

They both ask about you every time we see them. Judge has a very high opinion of you doing exactly right under all circumstances. Many asked about you at church. Mrs Sampson said some of them were going to write to you to keep you from being homesick. Jim Stinson telephoned Sunday afternoon for your address, said he was going to direct to Rev. C. S. Roberts.

Yesterday -- Tuesday -- afternoon I went with Mrs. McLean to make some calls. I was out at Mrs Mood's but she was not at home. She telephoned me this morning, asked after you. Says she thinks you are a fine boy. You see your little attentions recently have been appreciated. Last night Kirtley and I went to Mrs. Muse' for a little visit. When we left Margie said "When you write to Stanly give him my best". I thanked her and told her it would be appreciated. I am so anxious to hear about Princeton, your room, the profs-- & c & c. What your impressions are, and how you think you will like it. I would like if you can, that you should study Shakespeare, not to the exclusion of other literature, but see if you cannot study it also. It will be nice to have most of your time well occupied. I would like for you to appreciate and have some knowledge of Shakespeare. Both Maude and Margie are studying him.

Dr. Taylor is here, will be here about ten days. I have not

seen him yet. Tell me something about the weather, whether it is as cold there as it was the last morning you were here? If you would write on both sides of the paper you would save postage Charlie has just given me a rigmarole of a message for you something about praying for you and hoping for your <u>excess</u>. Goodbye.

With much love,

Mamma

Dinner Time --

Dear Stanly

Mama told me as soon as I came in, she had written you & left a page or more for me. I told her I had written and mailed you a letter this morning, however I would fill up the empty pages with something. As I suggested a Diary this morning Mama dont think you will have time, but suggests that to keep the Expense account would be proper.

I want to add Emphasis to what Mama says about reading.

I have just done a trade with old Uncle Bob (the Darky that wet up all the mortar for the Lowbridges when they built foundation of my house) to split up and & house all my wood -- put the chunks in my cellar -- I will have my coal hauled in four days & get ready for winter.

Dr. Moore has written for Dr Gevurent to come & hold a meeting in town, commencing first Sabbath-- Dr. G-- wrote that *he could come in Nov-- I had a letter from Irene a few days ago -- She wants to get a place in Land Office in Austin Tex -- and wants me to see some political friends of the probable in coming Land Commissioner. I have seen C. Smith and he said he would help her, all he could. Don't you mention this -- I fear there will be poor chance, as there will be good many applicants, I am sure --*

*I do not know what Henry is doing we haven't heard from him since you left. I think he must have gone to the county to pick cotton.*

*Well I must cut short & go up town. I have to go out with Secretary Committee this P.M. on the Cotton Scheme -- It is an unpleasant business, nearly everyone you ask says "I don't believe it will do any good" "money thrown away & c" -- There is but very little of a spirit of co-operation or <u>acting together</u> -- and it is getting worse every year -- and it will do more to kill Sherman than anything else.*

*Here I go for up town -- Good bye. Write often -- with much love*

<u>*Your*</u> *Papa*

*P.S. We had a large S. School Sunday the A.C.* [Austin College] *boys went. I asked Hutton to take your place in taking up Collection -- John says he would ask every five minutes if we were ready to take it up.*

[This sheet in C.N.'s writing is folded in with the letter. It is probably from the now missing letter which C.N. referred to having written earlier.]

*of energy into everything. Don't get into habit of sleeping late in*

September, 1898                                                              19

the morning -- One or two hours study in the morning is fine -- remember all Sherman is looking with a good deal of interest to your success -- Friends of Austin College will take great pleasure in getting it out that one of her Graduates entered Senior Class at Princeton and carried off some of the latters honors, if perchance such should be the case --

    Take great care of the <u>Physical body</u>, for sound robust health and strength there will constitute so much and largely to you <u>mental development</u> --

    Are you allowed to control your own finances -- or do they require you to turn your money over to the School Treasurer.

    We have a meeting of the Home Missions Committee this afternoon. Mr. Hartin is to be here -- I will have to stop as our meeting is at four o clock -- Dr Moore preached to the young people last night, from Text 1st Cor 12th Chap 31st v first clause "But covet earnestly the best gifts" -- It was one of his best sermons, wish you could have heard it -- All the College boys I think were out -- and all the <u>"kids"</u> I think -- not many of the <u>"Nash"</u>. One of the kid girls fainted and fell on the sidewalk after leaving church, at Dr Moore's corner -- It produced quite a sensation. She was taken to College unconscious, have not heard from her today, trust she is all right.

    Good bye -- Write about everything & often with much love

    Your Father

    C N Roberts

## THE THIRD LETTER

From C.N. in Sherman
23 September 1898

For this letter to his son, C.N. used the business letterhead of an earlier company: "The Roberts, Hardwicke & Taylor Co. Wholesale Hardware Sherman, Texas". The envelope featured a drawing of a gun and the words: "The Winchester Repeating 'Take Down' Shotgun For Sale by Roberts, Sanford & Taylor Co., Sherman Texas". The letter was addressed to Stanly's new residence: C.S. Roberts Esq. 148 Nassau St. Princeton NJ. This building is still standing and as a business near the corner of the campus it presents a charming old fashioned aspect. It does not take a lot of imagination, however, to see it as it may have appeared to any Senior in 1898 who would have been inclined to slightly compare it with the more elegant on campus housing.

This letter throws light on the interesting business practices of one hundred years ago. Although delay payments were not formalized with credit cards, many of the people who shopped at such stores as that run by C.N. Roberts bought on credit. At the end of each month (or quarter, depending on the type of the account) store employees wrote to customers asking for bills to be settled. Often these letters were termed "rounding up" letters. The candid manner in which C.N.

wrote to his son about the family business was a recurring theme in his letters to his future business partner.

C.N. veiled his candor a trifle, however, when he wrote adjuring his son to go no where he "could not take your Mother with you -- you understand what I mean". What Stanly was to understand from this was a warning against visiting prostitutes. In many ways the sexual mores of one hundred years ago were looser than our own. Although figures are difficult to produce, there were many times more prostitutes then than now and most college boys were expected to frequent the more "respectable" city brothels. Women's magazines hinted at the signs of syphilis a woman should look for in a man before agreeing to marry him and men's magazines carried pages of advertisements for "cures". What C.N. called "the mark" which would be carried "to the day of his death" and "poison his posterity" was a reference to the venereal diseases which were reaching epidemic proportion in the late 1890's.

That C.N. could both warn his son against sexual promiscuity and advise him on where to buy a glass of milk on Broadway is a reminder that although C.N. was a businessman in a small Texas town, the wholesale portion of his business kept him well-informed about the larger world; buying and selling trips had given him a wide travel experience. In this letter C.N.'s reference to being "out front" means that he was helping wait on customers in the retail section of the business rather than at his usual work of directing inventory purchase and managing the wholesale promotion, which was known as "jobbing" sales.

The "Ed" mentioned in this letter was C.N.'s brother, Ed Roberts who, like their brother Wallace's widow, and other Roberts family members, still lived in Connecticut, where C.N. had been born. Although their differing sides in the war had divided the Roberts brothers in the 1860's, family relations were cordial by the time Stanly was at Princeton.

This letter provides a reminder of how our learning about local news has changed. Although Sherman is now much more populous than it was in 1898, Sherman now shares one daily newspaper with Denison and other communities. In the 1890's Sherman had two of its own daily newspapers, the Register and the Democrat.

*Sherman Tex Sept 23/98*

*Dear Son:*

*I am seated at your table. Grace is reading under the light in our room. Mama is in the Library waiting for Dr Taylor who told me yesterday he would call to night -- it is 20 minutes of Eight. We have had a warm day and rather a busy one at the store. John has been very busy writing all day. I gave him nearly 100 letters to write <u>"rounding</u> up" letters before Oct 1st. Our Total Sales last month were nearly 21000, that was pretty good. Jobbing Sales ran over last year 6000. Retail fell off some.*

*Keenor has been off for a day or two got a boy at his house. Karne Hayden is helping Weems -- Weems dont like Karne much. He is too <u>plodding</u>. Cope is not back yet think he will come in about Sunday. I miss him I feel much better satisfied with Cope or Dick -- Yesterday I was out front a good deal as they needed help. Well Dr Taylor came in & I stopped went down & let him in & we, Mama, Doctor & myself had a good visit, it is*

*September, 1898*

now nearly 10 oclk -- Dr says you must come to New York Thanksgiving, says all the students generally go home or somewhere else, and that you must run up & see him. Court will be with him, says they will probably have a College Foot Ball at New York -- believe Princeton & Yale -- of course -- I will give you his Home number -- <u>#113 West 40th St</u> -- put it down in your Memorandum Book. If you will, remember when you go into New York, if it is after 5 oclk you can go right to his home & find him. If you go up on the Pennsylvania Central, it will land you at 23rd St take the Street Car to Broadway transfer and go up Broadway to 40th St, go West I think 1 Block -- If you want to stop at a Hotel stop at corner Broadway & 31st St at the "Grand Hotel" -- You can get a good room there for 1.<u>00</u>, or even 75ct a day -- and there are Lunch Stand Rooms as well as Cafes all around there. Dont have to eat at the Restaurant connected with the Hotel as it costs too much -- I recollect I went into a Cafe just across the street from the Hotel on Broadway, had a cup coffee, some Fish Bread -- Glass Milk and in fact all I wanted for 30ct --

Well I have got off track. You are not going to New York soon & I will write something more interesting.

Kirtley calls Grace & I will walk over with her -- I dont intend to finish my letter to night. Mama mailed you one to day & I will mail this tomorrow. We were pleased with your home as you described it, but Mama wants to know just how everything is located in you room & c. I hope you will keep it tidy & nice. Keep your clothes hung up and in order, shoes nice & c. I neglected to suggest to you to put your money in a Bank or with Treasurer of University and check it out as you want it -- I will send you some more any time you want it dont fail to write in time and how much -- Dont carry anything but little change, or at least small amount, with you or in your room -- as you can check *it out of Bank when you need or want it --*

*I wrote the Thompson Girls at Litchfield Conn today that you were at P-- & that you would probably run up & see them xmas. They are my first cousins, and mighty nice, pleasant Girls. I believe I told you that they live by themselves, two Sisters, a little older than Kirtley and Irene, but a good deal like them --I mean in actions -- I also wrote Emma (Wallace's widow) that you might run up to Canaan and see them all. Of course you would not stay with them but go on up to Ed's -- and the other relatives.*

*I saw Dr Sampson today and he asked after you, says they will soon have 100 Boys -- says the Mess Club is a success -- and gives cheap Board -- Capt Wharton says that they have a "fine school"*

*Edwin Kidel told me to day that they had all they could take care of, about 175 Boarders. I sold him another Furnace (like ours) today. The Oil mill has started up finally & is going a good deal giving us a good deal shop work. Tennille is putting up about 200 feet Gala Iron Cotton Suction Pipe -- 15 in Dia -- I think I will get the order in a day or two for 25 Tanks 200 Bbls each --*

*Let me know if you dont get the Register and Democrat both regularly, Daily -- and after one month if you want both say so, if one will do say which you want -- both have about the same news. I like Democrat the best -- well I will close to night as it is about 11 oclk & finish tomorrow ---*

*Saturday morning 9 oclk. I came up getting to the store 8 oclk this morning. To show you how anxious Mama and even Charlie is to get your letters they both said, if there is one there you must send it down by first car. Mama says "As soon as you*

*September, 1898*

see that there is one Telephone me, then take it out to front of Store and read it there so you will not miss a car" -- this morning we did get one -- the one where you spoke of hazzing process of Freshmen & c -- I went out read it, sent it on first car & telephoned Mama it was coming. Kirtley is as much interested as Mama almost. She comes over to see & hear every morning. You must always remember her & Charley -- I went right over to Register & Democrat offices & gave them your address you ought to get both papers for one month from date of first (both were ordered same day) I read part of your letter to the Boys in front. Jim laughed a good deal over the <u>Hazing Process</u>.

As soon as I get the bill from Treasurer you speak of I will send you some more money. Mama and I made a pretty correct estimate of how much you had left from the $50.00 cash I gave you. I hit it exactly.

While I want you to exercise economy & prudence in all of your money matters -- as I feel it to be as much a part of your Education (when you are thrown upon your own resources and judgement as you are now) as any other part, yet I do not want you to stint yourself. I want you to make the most you can out of the one or two years you spend up there. I mean in the way of acquainting yourself with the world & people -- hence I do not think it a waste of money for you to go to N.Y. Thanksgiving -- or to go to Conn. or anywhere else as close by xmas -- or to Phila or Washington anytime you can, be sure any trip you make to associate with the best people. If you go to Washington go & see Col. A. H. Garland an old friend of mine --- see Judge Kane, Congressman Bailey or his Secretary "James" -- Call on Pres McKinley, you have a right to. If you go to Phila call at the <u>Am. S. S. Union</u> Headquarters. You know I am one of the <u>Honorary</u> Vice Pres -- Call & see N. & G. Taylors, Merchants & Co,

McDiston & Sons, Biddle Purchasing Co . & c. If you go to Baltimore, call on "Mathias, Ingram & Co" from whom we buy a good deal stamped ware, "Weir & Wilson" Commercial Brokers -- #14 West German St. When you go to New York, Go to Peck, Stow & Wilcox Co. Call for <u>Col Wakley</u> the manager whom I met So Hdw Associates & afterwards, such a pleasant old Gentleman. He will take you to the Hardware Club.

    Call and see Adolph Kester & Co, Sargent & Co Call for Mr Sargent tell him who you are at Kester Bros call for Mr. Lipman you will find him very pleasant. Call at Winchester Arm Co call for Mr Hildreth or Irby Bennett if they should be in city, either of them, they would be very kind to you --- Be sure in any or all of the cities you visit to go no where that you could not take your Mother with you -- you understand what I mean -- "there is a gate that leads to Hell" <u>it</u> <u>is</u> <u>always</u> <u>wide</u> <u>open</u> -- if entered <u>however</u> <u>cautiously</u>, very often proves to be a <u>living</u> <u>Hell</u> to a young man, he carries the mark of it with him to the day of his death -- he would give the world to heal the wound, but no it stays with him, and often poisons his posterity a word here of caution from one that loves you as the flesh of his flesh and bone of his bone I hope will ever ring in your ears if ever tempted <u>and</u> <u>you</u> <u>certainly</u> <u>will</u> <u>be</u> for no young man <u>ever</u> <u>escapes</u> <u>the</u> <u>temptation</u>. He is just as sure to meet it as was the innocent guileless Joseph -- then my Boy remember this -- I hope and really believe so much in your love for both of us particularly your Mother that you will come back as pure as you left us -- our earnest daily prayers follow you.

*I must close --- so good bye -- Write us often and about everything. Boys all send best regards. With much Love*

*Your Father*

*C N Roberts*

**THE FOURTH LETTER**

From C.N. in Sherman
27 September 1898


For those familiar with the Roberts House as an historic house museum this letter brings a mist to the eyes with the images it invokes of the time when the mansion was a family home: Charlie "grunts" but comes to work, Knowles cuts the grass, the cat on the back porch meows -- and from one floor away C.N. hears the click of those still very audible light switches!

News of the world is as present as news of the home in this letter: the place where Sherman boys Leslie Moxey and Wallace Wilkins "had a tough time" was in the Spanish American War.

Although the beginnings of the Spanish-American War were in the Ten Years War in Cuba, 1868-1878, and the resulting independence movement and 1895 insurrection, the immediate cause is usually considered to be the 15 February 1898 explosion of the USS Maine in Havana Harbor. Although rumors have persisted for over one hundred years that the Maine was blown up by the United States herself in order to create American hatred of Spain, the 28 March report of the US Naval Court of Inquiry declared that the Maine was willfully destroyed by Spain. The following day the United States issued an ultimatum to Spain to leave Cuba and the phrase "Remember the Maine" entered the national vocabulary. On 1 April Spain replied, refusing to withdraw. On the 11th, President McKinley requested the Congress to vote permission for the US military to "intervene". The House and Senate voted to do so, but added the proviso that America must never try to control Cuba, just aid the Cubans in throwing off Spanish rule.

The mechanics of war were in place quickly and on 1 May US Commodore George Dewey made his famous remark, "You may fire when you are ready, Gridley." A mere six hours later and the entire Spanish squadron had been sunk. The immediate goal of the War seemed almost accomplished but, as history shows repeatedly, easy victories often fuel a lust for expanding power: the President ordered Spain to vacate not only Cuba but also Manilla and the US Fleet was ordered to Manilla. Private instructions to the fleet were that en route to Manilla, Guam should be captured.

Although the Spanish possession of the Philippine Islands had not been in question at the onset of the hostilities relating to the Spanish presence in Cuba, on the 18th of May President McKinley ordered a military expedition to the Philippines to "provide security" to the inhabitants by "occupying the islands and eliminating the Spanish forces". The first US troops arrived at the Philippines on 1 June 1898; the Marines landed at Guantanamo in Cuba on 10 June. Meanwhile back home the President urged "annexation" of Hawaii to "help get our share of China".

The majority of informed Americans were horrified by the aggressive actions and the American Anti-Imperialist League gained widespread support. Andrew Carnegie and Mark Twain were two of the League's most illustrious members. The United States' standing military and the 125,000 volunteers had a wretched time in all ways. Not only were the fighting conditions brutal but, in a scenario that sounds painfully familiar to those who remember the War in Viet Nam, American troops were reviled by the people they thought would laud them as liberators and at home the young men were often openly jeered at. No one had yet coined the important term, "Support the Troops, Oppose the Policy".

At least in 1898 the War and subsequent occupation were mercifully short. The peace treaty between the United States and a completely vanquished Spain regarding Cuba, Guam, Puerto Rico and the Philippine Islands was concluded before the end of June, although the United States also claimed Wake Island in January 1899. The period of occupation is considered to have ended in 1902. 4,200 young American lives had been sacrificed -- and between Spanish bullets and American bullets, over 200,000 civilians had been killed in the contested areas.

*Sherman Tex*
*Tuesday Sept 27th 1898*

*Dear Son:*

*I am seated at your table in your room at Dinner hour. Mama sitting by your East window -- one oclk whistle (Dedrick's) just blowing -- Your letter written Friday night came this morning -- We have just read it over the second time. We were both glad that your entrance into the Senior Class has been settled -- and now say -- for <u>the honors</u> -- at least some of them --*

September, 1898

*Mama wants to know if it will not be possible for you to study the French Language in some other class, and there would be a help in keeping up with French Literature of the Senior Class. She wants you to be sure & study French ---. Papa says -- Dont <u>forget</u> your Latin either. May not be able to stay in Latin but dont forget it.*

*We are glad to know that you are pleased with your home -- We hope you will endeavor to act well your part to make yourself a desirable member of the family -- use everything in your room and about the place with the utmost care -- and be particularly neat & nice -- In meeting and making arrangements, study to be pleasant, agreeable, unselfish --- and above all sincere -- <u>firm</u> <u>in</u> <u>your</u> <u>convictions</u> as to <u>right</u> & <u>wrong,</u> <u>be</u> <u>as</u> <u>true</u> as was Joseph -- I now have to go up to the store and will try to finish my letter then this evening -- Kirtley enjoyed hearing your letter read & says for you to write more about College Life -- I saw Leslie Moxey to day he looks fine, he has been discharged you know -- I also saw Wallace Wilkins -- he looks fine too -- He is going to try to get a discharge -- Tom is with Lyons Co. he wants to come home but Judge would rather he would stay -- so he told me this morning -- Wallace & Leslie both say that they had a tough time, say part of the time treated like animals -- Rowin Mills is at home and doing his best to get a discharge. All the Grayson Rifles are here on Furlough. Gus Tunner is buying cotton at Whitewright for Birge Forbes & Co- Dr Taylor starts back to New York to night -- so if you conclude to go to New York better wait & go up there when he is there --*

*9 1/2 oclock P.M. Here I am seated again at your table just where I got up from after dinner, and going up town, and Mama is down in the Library alone reading her book -- I found so much to do up town this afternoon that I could not finish your* letter -- I had a large list of remittances to get off, Ledlow & Parr working on statements -- Before Mama & I were through supper tonight, in came Maud Lilly and Legrand. Mrs Wood & her two cousins (Lady visitors) drove on below -- but in a little while they all drove back & all got out & all came in and sat with with [sic] us for an hour or more.

We had a nice visit all asked after you and Mrs Wood expresses herself as so glad that you had entered Senior Year at Princeton --

Dr Taylor came in & bid me a good bye late this evening -- starts back to New York this evening. He told me to write to you to be sure to come right to his office or room upon your arrival in N.Y. when you went there, from 1/2 past 9 to about 4- he would be at his office -- 111 5th Ave, between 16 & 17th Sts -- the balance of time at his home #113 West 40th St -- He said he wanted you to stay with him, that he had plenty room when Count was away -- or when he was there either as far as that was concerned, of course *you* can exercise your pleasure but it would be nice for you to stay with him, if there only one night -- or such a matter -- at all events be governed by circumstances, if he should insist strenuously would stay with him as he might conclude you did not appreciate his kindness as well as Company. He is such a warm & choice friend ours --

Mr Murphy is in New York & will be for some time. I dont know what Hotel he stops at -- I saw it in the Dallas News a few days ago.

Jo Etta is out rusticating this week claims his health is bad -- in fact does look badly -- We are having the most disagreeable weather now and have had it for two weeks, so hot *in the middle of the day, in fact nearly all day -- May Fairchild told me yesterday that his thermometer had registered 91 from 11 to 2 for a week -- A great many people are complaining. Charlie has been grunting although he has shown up every day -- Mrs Galloway's health is very bad Mama says -- she was there this afternoon -- Mr Knowles cut off the yard today, it needed it badly -- Mama & I went down to Mrs Taylors's last night -- and spent two or three hours --*

*We are all the time thinking about you and we wonder just how the introduction and getting acquainted with all the many students and also Professors suits you and you suit them, hope in the one year (if no more) you will make many a friend and acquaintance that will be a great pleasure to you in the future -- of course it will not be like you were going to be there for a four or five year course --*

*You have never mentioned getting any letters from us -- but we presume you have before this as one of us has written nearly every day except Sunday -- perhaps we have missed one or two days --*

*Well Mama has turned off lights downstairs -- hear them click and here she comes upstairs & says I am going to bed, that means it is late, & I will have to stop for this time -- The old cat is making the back porch ring with that old cry for "some meat" --*

*It is very still and warm tonight -- I have just been down & looked at the Thermometer in the Library -- it is 20 minutes of 11 oclk and registers 81 1/2 -- I am going to bed -- will leave my letter & in the morning finish it before breakfast -- so good night.*

*Wednesday morning 7 1/4 oclock. Another bright &*

pretty morning, considerable cooler. Temp on Porch 66 -- but will be another hot day. Charley will ring the bell in a minute or two for he knows I am up as I went down to see the Thermometer -- here it is -- so we are off for breakfast. After breakfast & prayers -- Charley had cake this morning, then at prayers we read 12 chap Isaiah <u>one</u> <u>of</u> <u>your</u> <u>favorites</u> (<u>because</u> <u>it</u> <u>is</u> <u>Short</u>) We are reading Isaiah by course -- We wonder if you and your Bible have prayers every morning -- Well -- here it is again I have got to go up town, Mama says -- and so I have -- must go out go out & see Mr Knowles, as I want him to clean up back yard where we had & sawed wood as well as to Line our Sewer Ditch -- so here goes will finish my letter up town --

At store & mail disposed of -- got some collection this morning -- nearly $1000. and some good orders -- We need the former & latter are very acceptable -- Everything as quiet as a funeral this morning -- everybody says it is going to be a hot day -- so it is -- I hand you herewith Mr Geo Murphys N.Y. address --

If you were to go to Philad -- and call at American S.S. Union Headquarters remember you are a <u>Life member</u> at the association -- also that Biddle Pen Co has an office there #1022 Arch St -- Mr C. M. Biddle himself stays there -- Well I must quit, burn up my letter when you have read for I dont want anybody to see such a mess -- I wouldn't dare to read it over myself, for if I should I believe that I would burn it myself -- Good bye -- with much love your PaPa

C. N. Roberts

## THE FIFTH LETTER

From C.N. and Emma in Sherman
29 September 1898

This is another letter in which the local and the national, the personal interest and the interest of world are charmingly blended. News of the oleanders and roses at the Roberts house vie for place with rumors of the trouble in the Grayson Rifles Regiment. Comments on Stanly's studies contain passing references to two of the Princeton community's most prestigious residents, both of whom would become known to Stanly. Stanly was taught by professor Woodrow Wilson and Stanly would frequently speak with former First Lady Frances Folsom Cleveland.

Stanly took seven classes each semester his year at Princeton with each class meeting twice a week. Students were expected to attend all three recitations or lectures held on Mondays, Tuesdays, Thursdays, and Fridays, and the one held Wednesday morning and the one held Saturday morning. At graduation, seventy seven members of the class admitted to having "cut" so many classes that on at least one occasion in his college career he had been summoned before a faculty committee. Stanly however, the earnest newcomer, rarely missed a class session.

I am grateful to Susan Hamson, Daniel Santamaria and Rosemary Switzer of the Seeley G. Mudd Manuscript Library of Princeton University for allowing me to view the material I needed to reconstruct Stanly's course schedule. The following quotations from the 1898-9 catalogue appear here with the kind permission of Princeton University Library and I am grateful to Daniel Linke, Princeton University archivist, for granting the request.

-- "Constitutional Government, its nature, genesis, and operation. Lectures and collateral reading." It was taught by Woodrow Wilson who was described in the student handbook as "Ph.D., LL.D. McCormick Professor of Jurisprudence and Politics." The textbooks used in the course were listed as STUDIES IN CONSTITUTIONAL LAW by E. Boutmy, and Wilson's own book, THE STATE.

-- "History: Modern European History with special references to the consolidation of the German states" taught by John Haughton Coney, A.M., Assistant Professor of History.

-- "English Literature. Poets from Cowper to Browning, Prose writers Scott, Carlyle, Landor, Thackery, De Quincey, Jane Austen, Charlotte Bronte and George Eliot." It was taught by "the Dean and Mr. Tuckeman." The Dean of the college was James Ormsbee Murry, DD. LL.D., "Holmes Professor of Belles Lettres and English Language and Literature."

-- "Poetics: Lyric, narrative and dramatic poetry will be studied as forms of expression." This was taught by Bliss Perry, A.M. "Professor of Oratory an AEsthetic Criticism"

-- "Biblical Literature, the History of the Jews" taught by "John Grier Hibben, Ph.D, Stuart Professor of Logic and T H P Sailer

Assistant in Biblical Instruction."

-- "French Literature of the Eighteenth Century, Beaumarchis, Voltaire, etc." Students were alerted that there would be copious reading in French of the novelists, the dramatists and in the area of recent criticism. The course was taught by "Arnold Guyot Cameron, Ph.D. Professor of French."

-- Theism. It was impossible to determine which course Stanly took in this division, which is a shame, as he later reported it was the only class first semester in which he made "first group" in the finals, meaning that he was in the top twenty percent of the class.

*Thursday Afternoon*
*Sept. 29 -- 1898*

*Dear Son,*

*I intended writing this morning but while out in the yard doctoring an oleander for scales, Mrs. Williams came for some flowers, and wanted me to go this afternoon to a funeral (benevolent funeral).*

*It took me a long time to get through with the oleander, and as it was a nice cloudy morning I spent the balance of it watering flowers, knowing I could not do it this afternoon. It will soon be time for Mrs. Williams to come so I will no more than get my letter started. I asked lots of questions in my last letter, but not half as many things as I want to know. I want you to imitate Papa in writing details and think up all you can for there is nothing that will not interest us.*

Dr Moon has not been well for a week or more -- suffering with neuralgia -- So Dr. Sampson lead prayer meeting for us last night. We had a good talk on "What doest thou here Elijah"? After the service Dr. Sampson took me by the arm saying, "So <u>our boy</u> got there"!

You have the credit of Austin College on your shoulders, so do it honor. So many are surprised that you could enter the Senior Class. I want the Princeton profs also to feel that they made no mistake in allowing you this privilege. I hope you realize what a nice thing it is to have this opportunity for improvement and will make the most of it.

*Friday 30*

Mrs. Igo came for me to go with her to Mrs. Galloways I could not go, so she remained with me until Mrs. Williams came for me. It was cloudy and the drive was very pleasant. I went to Mrs. Galloway's as soon as I returned, found Mrs. Igo still there. Mrs. Galloway told me to always remember them to you. I intended finishing my letter last night but it was a beautiful moon light night and papa was in the humor for going to Mr. Dillard's. We had a very pleasant visit there and propose going to Mrs. Finley's to night if it is pleasant.

There is thick fog this morning almost like rain. I have just received your nice letter. I told papa when he spoke of a diary that your letters would make a good diary. I am very much delighted with the drawing. I know now just how you are located. I think you have been very moderate in your expenses. Papa will send you some money soon. We want you to have what you need.

September, 1898

*Your letter was very interesting. I like to have you go into detail and tell about everything. And everything about your studies and profs. will be of the utmost interest. I am glad you have a lesson under Prof. Wilson. We hardly thought we would get a letter before tomorrow morning but I told papa to telephone any way whether he received one. So I was much delighted when he said there would be one down on the next car. I read it to Charlie and then sent it to Kirtley. I may take it over to Judge & Mrs. Galloway to read. I am glad you have a real Frenchman for a teacher and that you like him. How do you feel now about being at Princeton. Do you feel it was a wise thing to do. I hope you will join the Philadelphian Society -- if it is a good one – and take an <u>active</u> part in it. I want you to present the letter that Dr. Moore wrote for he will want to hear from it. Leslie Maxie came to see me the other afternoon, he looked real well and not so very brown. He thinks Col. Rich responsible for most of the trouble in their regiment, he did not want to leave his pretty wife. Leslie is going back to Purcell, says he has nothing in view but thinks he will stand a better chance there than here. Mrs. Lee Woods, Maude and their visitors were here one evening this week. Mrs. Wood continues to say nice things about you. I had a nice long letter from Bet last night.*

*Rose is married and gone to live in Southern Miss. She writes so much about fishing, seems to enjoy it so much. Asked about you, do not know that you have gone to Princeton. They are very anxious for us to come out on a visit.*

*My roses are doing nicely. Mrs. Galloway has some very handsome ones. I am going to take some cuttings from them next month. Kirtley sends love and says "gather the rosebuds while you may" in other words, get all the profit and pleasure you can, says* she would like to have some of the nice walks. Is not the Philadelphian Society an Episcopalian organization? It seems to me I remember reading about it in the Catalogue.

Have you seen where the Clevelands live? How are they liked in Princeton? I hope you will not need any 'cuts' -- I am so anxious for you to form a taste and love for books -- real good literature -- I hope you can do or take up more or less in the line of your studies. What part of the Bible will you study?

Tell me something about the 'politics' when you write, also about the teacher. What division of your class are you in?

I went to see Mrs. Parks the other morning. She is up and around but not able to do anything. They are without help -- all in the cotton field -- So Mr. Parks has his hands full between home and the store.

Do people _place_ you as Southern by your language? Practice, try to acquire elegance in expressing yourself and avoid everything slouchy. You will think we give a great deal of advice, but we are so interested. Dr. Taylor left Wednesday he wanted to get back by the 1st of Oct. Mr. Galbraith came into prayer meeting Wed- night with Miss Hockerty. He seems partial to tall girls. They came in late and Miss Ela looked quite conscious. Papa has come for dinner, he said Mrs. Sampson was in and said they had a letter from you an enjoyed it so much. Take much pains with the letters you write to others. The one I received this morning was so nicely written. Be sure to study as hard or harder than if you had to answer questions. You will then profit by what you learn and be prepared for examinations. They have the lectures at the Austin University. We are both so much pleased with your letter. Hope your throat is quite well.

*Lovingly*

*Mamma*

*Stanly:*

*Mr Purnell a travelling man representative for Merchant & Co, of Philadelphia, a Gentleman that has been here two or three times a year for several years & one I like right well -- told me yesterday that he had a cousin, an Asst. Prof. at Princeton, "Asst. Prof. of Math". His name is Harry Covington, he was anxious for you to meet him -- I promised to write you. I have no time to write you more now -- will try to keep up my end in writing however & write you tomorrow.*

*Your Father*

*C N Roberts*

## THE SIXTH LETTER

From Emma in Sherman
Early December 1898

Sadly there are no surviving letters from either side of the corresponding parties for October and November, but this letter, postmarked on December 9th, continues in the same strain as the previous letter in this collection.

*Friday 7-20 A.M.*

*My Dear Sonny*

*I am beginning early, before breakfast, by electric light, Mrs. Sutherland has not come out of her room. It is a dark morning, the ground is covered with snow, and it still comes down in fine particles. I have an engagement with Miss Mollie this morning but feel doubtful about trying to get there. You will think from my frequent talk about the dress maker that I am well supplied, but I have only gotten one dress made as yet.*

*Mrs. and Mr. Erwin are to come tomorrow afternoon and stay over Sunday, the weather prospect is very bad now, I am wondering how it is with you. Noon. Mrs. Sutherland and I*

*December, 1898*

*spent the morning in the library, talking and reading. We have just come up stairs, and she is writing with a pencil to Mrs. Inge Miss Mollie telephoned me not to come this morning. If any letter came from you this morning papa did not telephone me. He went up town quite late. If I do not get a letter I will know it is on account of the examinations. If the weather is very bad Christmas, I want you to consider your health before everything else. It will not do to risk that for sightseeing. Pneumonia or something else serious would be a poor recompense. I think you can visit the New England relatives a little while in the summer before coming home. If it should be too bad to go to Washington during the Christmas holidays you can also go there next summer. It continued to snow and look gray all the morning, but now it is nearly clear. I suppose we will have a good slushy Sunday. Two snows before Xmas is, as you know, rather unusual.*

*The main thing in being away from your room in severe weather would be the having a comfortable bed and room. Papa came to dinner bringing a letter. He said he had to walk up this morning and that the cars were very irregular.*

*I am very proud of your 'excellent' in Poetics. Send me the next paper in Poetics also.*

*Mrs. Sutherland thinks with me that there would certainly be enough in Washington to interest you for a few days. If Dr. Taylor invites you up N.Y.* [words "*I would*" are crossed out] *You must certainly not go unless agreed that you should board yourself. Mrs. Sutherland is on one side of the table writing to Bert and I am on the other writing to you but both of our tongues wag much faster than our pens. What kind of night gowns have you? If they are not warm I could make you a couple of Outing cloth and send them to you.*

*I have just finished the third volume of my English history. I thought of you while reading about the Elizabethan period of literature and felt like discussing it with you. How did you like the one book you read by Jane Austen. Tell me what you read of the other authors. Mrs. Sutherland says she and Bert have laid off to read a good deal of Dickens, Scott, and Shakespeare this winter. We are going to read one of Shakespeare's plays when we finish our letters. At the rate we are writing dark will catch us. Mrs. Sutherland will probably only be with us until after Christmas.*

*I sent off for some books -- poems -- for my class, and some novels for the Darnalls for Christmas. I waded over to Mrs. Galloway's this afternoon and carried her two of your Warner books. She seems to like them. She wanted to come over yesterday afternoon but when she found Mrs. Sutherland was here she would not come. I have not heard a word from Bet. I mailed a letter to Carrie yesterday. You must not write to Dr. Taylor unless he writes to you, but of course you wont, I do not want you to be any more expense to him. Count Jones is coming home Christmas. We will miss our boy but we want him to have a good time. Papa will send you some money before long I wonder how much you will need.*

*Lovingly Mamma*

## THE SEVENTH LETTER

From Stanly at Princeton
10 December 1898

Stanly had a good bit of fun while at Princeton in studying (and occasionally exploiting) the Yankee's credulous misconceptions about Texans. In this letter Stanly shared with his parents some of the more amusing regional differences he encountered, as well as a myth he was enjoying perpetrating!

*Saturday 4 P.M.*

Dear <u>Folks</u>

*I have written two letters already this week so I wont write but a very short one this afternoon -- your Monday letter received Thursday --*

*We have been having pretty cold weather here, 24 - 32, for the last two or three days. It looks like it might snow about tomorrow. Up in N.Y. about Buffalo the snow is four feet deep -- trains stopped -- and a cold time generally. Yes people here know what persimmons are. They grow up here in some places. They dont know what okra and hot tamales are and you might as well* talk Dutch to them to say two "bits" instead of twenty five cents

I have about $20.00 left of that last $30.00. I never have paid any laundry bill yet. I guess they will collect all at once sometime. I dont know how much my Christmas trip will cost me --

Our Thanksgiving dinner was very "swell" -- We had twelve courses and were at the table nearly two hours.

The New York Journal said yesterday that there was a blizzard coming this way from the west and all that would keep it from reaching would be the fact that it might be broken up by a cyclone that has been "generated" over "Texas" and was also coming this way --

Did you see anything of the latter --

I have got the people up here believing that we have a cyclone regularly once a week and that we take one every Friday just like we would have a bath every Saturday. Did I tell you about the boy in Gettysburg -- I was looking at some old pistols in the museum when the man asked me where I was from. I told him Princeton N.J. but that I lived in Texas. The hotel boy who was with me, backed off a little and said "Well you are used to them things aint you?" -- Of course I said I was --

The man at the hotel asked me to register because I was from "a good ways off" --

Its getting dark (Its only 4-30) so I must take this letter down to the P.O. and mail it or it wont leave here til Monday.

*Goodbye with lots of love*

*Stanly*

*P. S. Tell Charlie "Hello" for me -- Love to Judge & Mrs G-- Dr & Mrs Moore and all my friends*

*CSR*

**THE EIGHTH LETTER**

From Stanly at Princeton
13 December 1898

    Because of the frequency with which both Stanly and his parents wrote their letters, there are often several letters between a question being asked and a question being answered. In this letter Stanly answered earlier questions from his mother about his health and about his night wear. And with the answers two of Emma's fears were realized: Stanly <u>did</u> get "la grippe" while away from her care, and he <u>was</u> picking up modern ways of living. The young man had discarded nightgowns and was wearing the more fashionable pajamas which he had bought for himself. It is probably safe to assume that in the small matter of pajamas rather than a nightgown for her son Emma's supportive interest in all the new things which Stanly was experiencing outweighed her general dislike of old ways being abandoned.

Princeton N. J.
Dec 13th '98
1-P.M.

Dear Folks

I would have written yesterday on my regular day but as I had written Saturday I thought I would wait until to day --

Well I have had a new experience -- have been sick and had the Dr. and gotten well again all in the space of two days --

I had the "Grippe". Out of the ["eight" crossed out] nine people who eat at our table six of us have had it and nearly all of us about the same time and exactly the same thing. My case was the shortest however. Sunday morning I woke up with a sore throat but otherwise felt all right until about ["twelve" crossed out] nine o'clock. Then I had a regular "busting" headache set in. I went to church in the morning however but in the afternoon I didnt do anything much but sit around and hold my head in my hands. About four I decided to go down and see a Dr so I went down and called on Dr Wright. He felt of my pulse, said I had fever, looked at my tongue, gave me two or three prescriptions and said now Mr Roberts you go home and go to bed at once and stay there til I come to see you tomorrow, which I proceeded <u>not</u> to do. I went home but I am not overly fond of going to bed in the daytime and so I propped myself up in my big rocking chair by the stove and talked to Mr Fulmer, the fellow that rooms next to me, -- I went to bed about eight oclock and kicked around all night. I think I kicked so much that I kicked off all my fever for the next morning when the Dr. came he found me sitting in my chair highly interested in a book Mr Fulmer loaned me. He said he didnt think I needed him anymore and I told him I didnt think so either. Dont get after me for not writing you and telling you I was sick for I got well before I had a chance to write.

Seems to me you all must be having some cold weather down there now.

I send you a little item which Mr Cook cut out of a Trenton (N.J.) paper to show me. If that slip is true you all have had a good deal colder weather than we have had for today is as cold a day as we have had at all and its only 24 here now.

I cant send the paper in poetics this time for there wasnt any only two or three questions on the board.

I have an examination in English Literature Friday morning. It is final and is the wind up of the Deans English for this time. I have been studying it a good deal today and I guess Quackenbush and I will study it together tonight.

I haven't heard any thing from Conn. yet. I think myself it will be rather cold up there Christmas. I have two weeks in June with nothing to do when I finish my exams, and think that would be a good time to visit up there.

I am glad Mrs Sutherland is with you all. Hope you will persuade her to stay a month or two. I dont need any night gowns. I wear pajamas. I bought them in New York when I was there. I like them better than night gowns they are in two pieces you know.

I read Northanger Abbey by Jane Austen. I liked it very well though there didnt seem to be much in it.

*December, 1898*

    *I have read Scarlet Letter Romola and Last Days of Pompeii. The only thing I have to read now is one of Trollopes.*

    *I got a letter from you both yesterday but have misplaced Papa's and cant find it. Have to stop now and go to French class so will say Goodbye with lots of love to you both also Mrs S.*

    *Stanly --*

## THE NINTH LETTER

From Stanly in Connecticut
31 December 1898

Despite his fears that a Christmas in Connecticut would be less appealing, weather wise, than June in Connecticut, Stanly went to his paternal Uncle Ed's for his Christmas break. During the holidays Stanly's Aunt and Uncle became ill and in helping his teenaged cousin, May, care for the house and for her parents Stanly grew quite fond of her. We usually focus on the sorrow of Stanly's parents in losing a nephew and two daughters, but Stanly knew that loss as well; he grew up in a house filled with pictures of three children who would have been his playmates. Perhaps that Christmas with May Stanly felt some of the companionship of a sibling that he may have often imagined when he was a child.

Like the good businessman he was to be for almost seventy years, Stanly also interested himself in his Uncle's business and, in fact, this letter was written on his Uncle Ed's business letterhead. Both the paper and envelope have printed on them: "East Canaan Co-operative Creamery Association Manufacturers of Gilt-Edge Butter and Cream E. S. Roberts, Secretary and Treasurer. East Canaan, Conn."

Enclosed with this letter was an exam page. Emma's life long thirst for knowledge compelled her to try to live vicariously through Stanly as he studied. As earlier letters show, she tried to read along with him and she wished him to send her copies of all of his reading lists, papers and tests. This surviving test paper gives wonderful insight into Stanly's course work. From what we know of their interests, it is probable that both Emma <u>and</u> Stanly would have been happier if it had been Emma who had had to take the exam!

*Dec 31st 1898*

*Dear "Folks": --*

*I guess you all think I have been very bad about writing letters but I will promise to do better next week. I honestly havent had time to write this week. This is not going to be much of a letter because I have only a few moments now. I have just finished <u>washing</u> & <u>wiping</u> the breakfast dishes and making up my bed and dusting the parlor etc. while May has been waiting on the invalids.*

*I have been afraid every day that May would get sick and then <u>goodness only knows</u> what we would do. You might think I am not having a good time but honestly I believe I have had a better time this week than anytime since I left home. Its the next thing to being at home to be here and it seems fine to be where I am "Stanly" again and not "Mr Roberts from Princeton". I am not certain just when I will get back to Princeton Wednesday or Thursday I dont know which -- I think I will go back there Thursday morning get there about 11 A.M. I guess I will leave* here Monday. I have been doing some bookkeeping for Uncle Ed and may do some more. I dont think I will go to see any of my other relatives this time. I will stay here and help May. I think I shall want to come back up here in May and if I do can go to the other places then.

I forgot to tell you Mifflin went to Cuba to spend the Holidays -- got two letters from Mrs Hood. One just before I left Princeton and another just after I got here.

Did I tell you what time I get up in the morning -- six o'clock, and some times a quarter before six --

Tell Kirtley I am ever so much obliged for the picture and that just as soon as I get a spare minute I will write her and thank her myself. Miss Irene sent me a pretty little needlecase and Tot Mattison sent me a little "business" to put my razor in.

How long is Mrs Sutherland going to stay with you. I think it was so nice for her to be with you Christmas -- Did I tell you that the weather here night before last was 2 below zero. Well today it is 53 above. Some difference isnt there. Today it is warm enough here to be Texas.

I am going to tell Uncle Ed that when I go home in June I think he ought to let May go with me. Wouldn't it be nice to have her spend the summer with us. Well I'll have to stop and see what I can do to help May --

Goodbye with lots of love

Stanly

1. State the fundamental ideas involved in a theistic as opposed to a pantheistic or materialistic theory of the universe.

2. State the leading opinions entertained as to the mode by which we arrive at the Theistic conception of the universe & defend your own view.

3. Give in outline an account of the course of theistic discussion from Thale to Kant.

4. The validity of the argument for the existence of God based upon the simple idea of causation. Show this & show also that the argument a contingentia mundi is a good one.

5. Defend the doctrine of final cause against those (a) who deny the fact of finality in nature and those (b) who address finality but deny the ordinary theistic references.

6. State under a proper scheme of classification the antitheistic theories, and dealing with the unphilosophical forms of antitheism state the leading forms of polytheism.

7. State and comment upon the leading questions connected with the philosophy of polytheism.

8. State the leading features in Spinoza's system and give your reason for regarding him as a pantheist.

9. Mention some of the prevailing forms of thought which have been unjustly charged with being pantheistic with the reasons you have for entertaining a contrary opinion.

10. Give some account of the history of materialism.

## THE TENTH LETTER

From Emma in Sherman
2 January 1899


Even the kindest people are victims of the prejudices inherent to the time and place in which they live. Emma gave unstintingly of her time and money to help the poor and the ill but, like all women of her era, she harbored some accepted prejudices which now repel us. The memory of the kindness with which she tended to those in need and the earnestness with which she enjoyed Ladies Aid and a week of prayer should not be marred for modern readers of her letters because she expressed then popular prejudices which we now know to be cruel and unfounded.

Paragraphing has been added to this letter which was written hurriedly in a block on several sheets of Roberts, Hardwicke and Taylor letterhead.

*Monday 9-45 A.M.*
*Jan 2nd <u>1899</u>*

*My Dear Son,*

*Friday afternoon Mrs. Sutherland and I had settled ourselves for a quiet afternoon at home when I received a telephone message to go and visit a sick family way down on Mulberry street, near the Depot. It was in Mrs. Darnall's ward but she was out of town and Mrs. Williams had grippe. So I took Mrs. Sutherland and we went out into a very cold disagreeable wind. As it was on the car line we soon arrived at the house.*

*A family by the name of Gray -- an old car driver -- They have had a great deal of sickness. She wanted some wood and groceries. We hunted a wood yard near by -- owned by a Mr. Dorherty -- when we knocked at the door and he presented himself. Behold, a picture from Dickens in real life! He was so ugly, and so shabby Mrs. Sutherland said he looked so villianous that she felt afraid to order the wood from fear he would not be honest. He was a very ugly Irishman and I never saw a better Dickens picture. I wish we could have had a 'snap shot' of him as he stood at the door. After we accomplished our errand we called on Mrs. McLean who is just recovering from Grippe.*

*Saturday we spent at home, not knowing on what train, or at what hour Mr. Bishop would come. About the middle of the Afternoon we received a telephone message saying he would be over about seven or later. Capt. R. said we had better wait supper, and so we did, until he telephoned us he was sure he would have eaten supper before starting and for us not to wait.*

*While Mrs. Sutherland and I were eating Mrs. Darnall*

and Kirtley came over to spend the evening. We had to take them upstairs as the minister came soon after. Mrs. Sutherland entertained them in your room, while I entertained the minister and papa ate his supper. We liked Mr. Bishop so much. He is a man of about thirty-eight but as he only wears a moustache he looks much younger.

As Capt. Roberts and I were walking to S.S. we were joined by Mr. Brent who told us there had been a wreck on the Central just this side of McKinney the night before at nine o'clock. He said there were a number of deaths. We were of course excited as there were a number of Sherman people known to be on the train, among them Dr. Sampson. We soon learned that the report was exagerated [sic] and that no one was killed and only one seriously hurt.

Later we heard that the one seriously hurt one was Mr. Galbriath. That when they left him at McKinney he was spitting blood and that Dr. Sampson was very apprehensive about him. Papa got Dr. Erwin of McKinney and learned that he was well taken care of at Mrs. Hurd's and that he was some better. Quite a number were jolted up and bruised but not seriously hurt. Dr. Sampson was one of this number. He was bruised and lame and could not preach for Mr. Bishop -- as intended -- consequently Mr. Bishop felt that he must return to his church at night.

Mary Boyd, and a cousin, were left in McKinney, not seriously hurt, but the Dr. thought Mary had better not return at once. Mrs. Boyd went down yesterday. Prof. Rosebro was on the train but unhurt, also Mary Milton and Sedgewick and others. Grace and Bertha -- who are visiting their father -- were expected on the train, but it seems they did not come.

We didnt get our Dallas paper this morning. I do not know why. Yesterdays paper had very little in it. The accident occurred on or near same trestle two miles this side of McKinney. A loose rail derailed the engine and baggage car and the others smashed up against them. It is said to seem miraculous the immunity of the passengers.

Mrs. Sutherland and I went alone to teachers meeting. Papa was kept so busy telephoning about the wreck and trying to arrange things for Mr. Bishop and about service at our church at night that he did not go with us. He walked a great deal and was so tired that he did not go with us to church at night.

We had no service at our church so Mrs. S. and I went to hear the new Baptist minister. Yesterday was his first day as pastor. Jim Stinson and Frank Spangler acted as ushers. A great many Presbyterians were present. They went to our church expecting service and then came on to the Baptist.

This is the first Monday in the year so we will go to Ladies Aid at three o'clock and tonight to prayer meeting at our church. This is the week of prayer you know. I will stop now and perhaps add more tonight. It is clear and bright to day but tolerably cold.

We have just returned and it is six and as we go back to prayer meeting I will have very little time to write. Dr. Sampson says three cars went off on the right side of the trestle and three on the left side. One staid on the track. I suppose you will get the account in the city paper. The Miss Lee mentioned is a cousin of Mary Boid [sic], she was returning to school. She had three ribs broken and a cut under the eye.

January, 1899

*We received your scrap of a letter this afternoon. Are glad you are well and having a good time. Mrs. Sutherland is sitting by the table reading "Initials". She will return to Paris [Texas] Wednesday afternoon. Has been in Sherman over a month.*

*I wrote you one letter to East Canaan, this will go to Princeton. I hope you will feel like getting down to good work when you get back. Do you come in touch with any of your Profs? Do any of them know you personally? Mr. Bishop attended the Seminary at Princeton one year. Court returns to school in a few days, he has been having a good time with cousins from Houston.*

*With ever so much love*

*Mamma.*

## THE ELEVENTH LETTER

From Stanly at Princeton
9 January 1899

It is hard work for most college boys of any era to come up with topics about which to write home. Stanly claimed, at the beginning of this letter, that he had not "an earthly idea" what to write about and his letter does indeed flounder about for a bit. At last he hit on the idea of telling about his electives and this college news must have interested his parents.

Again, thanks to the resources carefully kept at the Seeley G. Mudd Manuscript Library at Princeton it is possible to learn about Stanly's courses his second semester. Again, I wish to express my gratitude to Princeton University Library and staff for permission to quote from the 1898-9 catalogue.

-- "The Elements of Economics. Lectures and Recitations." The text was POLITICAL ECONOMY by Hadley and it was taught by Walter Augustus Wyckoff, Assistant Professor of Political Economy.

-- "Ethics Theoretical and Practical, the formulation of moral obligation, the will, conscience, the nature of virtue, and the moral law." The textbook was HANDBOOK OF MORAL PHILOSOPHY by Calderwood and it was taught by the University President, "Frances Patton, DD. LL.D., Robert Lenox Professor of Biblical Instruction and Stuart Professor of Ethics and the Philosophy of Religion."

The other five courses were taught by professors under whom Stanly had also studied his first semester.:

-- "Oratory and Aesthetic Criticism: Prose Fiction. A study of prose fiction as a form of literary art" taught by Bliss Perry.

-- "American Constitutional Law. Lectures and collateral reading. [Texts] AMERICAN CONSTITUTIONAL LAW by Cooley and THE LAW OF THE CONSTITUTION by A. V. Dicey." Woodrow Wilson was the professor.

-- "Constitutional and Political History of England since the Reformation. Lectures and collateral reading." This was taught by John Haughton Coney

-- "French Literature of the Nineteenth Century, the Ethics of France and of French Literature" taught by Arnold Guyot Cameron.

-- "Prophetical Books of the Old Testament" taught by John Grier Hibben

*Monday*
*4-30 PM*

*Dear Folks:*

*I am beginning this letter without an earthly idea what to write about. There isnt a thing of interest I can tell you -- Your letter written Friday was received about a half an hour ago.*

*I smelt the violets the minute I opened the letter.*

*So you have all got the Grippe down there. We had most of ours before Christmas.*

*I see from the paper that it is all over Sherman.*

*I haven't received the paper yet but I will be very glad when it comes as I will need some soon. I came very near buying some today. I am glad now that I did not.*

*We have had two days of beautiful weather here but it is over now. Yesterday and today were both bright and warm regular spring days. We went all around without wraps but this afternoon it has clouded up and began to rain. It is still warm but it will probably turn cold tonight.*

*The winter is half over now according to the calendar but they say that February is the worst month here generally.*

*They certainly must be doing a big amount of work at the store. It is too bad that Keener is sick just at the time they need him most. If Harve gets the Grippe I do not see what on Earth they will do,*

*We have to hand in a list of electives we will take for next term to day. We have two required studies -- Ethics & Political Economy. Then we have to choose five electives beside -- I will take the same I have now except I will leave out Theism and English lit. in the place of the two required ones. The Prose Fiction I will take from Prof Perry really is English lit. The numbers below are the pages in the catalogue -- 2nd term then will be Prose Fiction page 53 -XI-6, Constitutional Law page 44-*

January, 1899                                                    65

*IV-2II, History, page 44-III-12 French page 96-8 Bible page 58 XVII-6 Political Economy page 93-2 Ethics page 39 I-2a.*

*You can read about each of these in the catalogue if you want to. I also send you a schedule of examinations with mine marked. You will see I have two on one day but as they are neither very hard I dont mind it very much. I send you also a piece about Mr Hood which I cut from the paper Mrs Hood sent me a day or two a go. The last picture of him is fine and looks just like him. Well I'll close for this time. <u>Lots</u> <u>of</u> <u>love</u> to both of you -- Goodbye --*

*Stanly R.*

## THE TWELFTH LETTER

From Stanly at Princeton
1 February 1899

In this letter Stanly again wrote news which would be of the most interest to his mother; he wrote about his courses and he included copies of three of his test papers. In light of his future Presidency and his work on the League of Nations it is of great interest to read Woodrow Wilson's test questions for his course.

It is also important to note the honor code at the bottom of each test paper which reads, "I pledge my honor as a gentleman, that, during this examination, I have neither given nor received assistance." Woodrow Wilson's <u>wife</u> is often credited with being a motivating force in having an honor code replace proctored tests at Princeton.

Mrs. Wilson was known to be a loving help to many classes of college students, offering a mixture of compassion and advice. She was particularly fond of Southern students and when, in 1892, two boys from Virginia told her how discouraged they were at the widespread cheating they saw occurring during proctored examinations she suggested they agitate for the creation of a honor system, similar to that used at William and Mary College in their home state. The boys stirred up so much interest on campus that the matter of an honor code came up for discussion at a faculty meeting in January of 1893. Woodrow Wilson leant eloquently support for the measure and by the beginning of the next school year the honor code replaced proctored examinations and it was widely believed that cheating almost disappeared.

*Feb 1st 11<u>45</u>*

*Just got back from <u>Theism</u> examination. Put two hours in it 9<u>30</u> -- 11<u>30</u>. It wasn't near so hard as I expected. Got through it all right. My hardest exam is over now and wasn't so hard after all. Guess you will get this letter about the same time you do the other one.*

*I did not mail the other one last night and it didn't get off until this morning. Next exam is English -- comes Friday morning. I have all day tomorrow to study for it. It will be principally writing essays. I don't suppose I will do particularly fine in it for I am very poor at essay writing, but there isn't any danger of my not passing it.*

*Then Saturday comes Poetics and then Monday comes History & French and then I am done for this term. New term begins Thursday Feb, 9th. Today is first day of February. Last month of winter. It snowed all last night, its three or four inches deep today -- but the sun is shining bright.*

*When I got up this morning the temperature was ten above zero. Now at 12 oclock it is 18 above. Well as this is the second letter today I'll stop. I just thought as I had a few spare* moments I would write and tell you about exams. Goodbye --

*Stanly*


EXAMINATION IN CONSTITUTIONAL GOVERNMENT
January 26, 1899


1. Is France a fully developed "constitutional" state? Give reasons for your answer.

2. What stages of "constitutional" government does the present political organization of Prussia illustrate?

3. Under what circumstances will the Government be most likely to be the leader of a progressive and developing nation? Give instances.

4. Is election the best process by which to pick out leaders under a "constitutional" government"? Give reasons and illustrate.

5. In what country is the imperative petition used? In what forms is it used there? What criticisms may be made of it as an instrument of political action?

6. Show the necessary limitations of "popular" administration and the proper field and most advantageous conditions of "expert" administration.

7. What are the advantages and what are the disadvantages of electing judges?

8. Why cannot a nation make rapid progress in freedom?

9. What are the various sources of English "constitutional" law and practice? (Boutmy)

10. How does the conception of sovereignty differ in France, England, and the United States? (Boutmy)

"I pledge my honor as a gentleman, that, during this examination, I have neither given nor received assistance."

EXAMINATION IN BIBLE
Junior-Senior Elective

1. Mention several incidents which illustrate Abraham's faith. Was there anything in his life which indicated a weakness of character?

2. Give an outline of the march from the wilderness to the Jordan. Why was a circuitous route taken? What battles were fought upon the way?

3. [no question]

4. Nature of the conquest of the Jordan? Give in general the chief characteristics of the period of the Judges. State the story of the Danites and the young Levite.

5. Describe Saul's campaigns against the Philistines. State some incidents which reveal the character of Jonathan.

6. Mention the different periods in David's life; also the main features of the reforms and progress of his reign.

7. What occasioned the division between Judah and Israel? What are the general

characteristics of the history of these two kingdoms?

8. In what way did the careers of two women affect [sic] the national character of Israel and of Judah? Who were the reformers in the history of Judah? What was the influence of the prophets in Israel and in Judah?

9. Describe briefly the several expeditions during the period of the Restoration.

10. What were the relations between the Jews and the Macedonian rulers? Give the chief features of the Maccabean dynasty.

"I pledge my honor as a gentleman, that, during this examination, I have neither given nor received assistance."


January 30, 1899
Princeton University Examination in Theism
February 1, 1899

1. State the Spencerian position as to the genesis of the theistic belief, with comments.

2. Sum up the results of theistic discussion in ancient philosophy, with special mention of leading names.

3. State the positions taken by Aquinas and Anselm respectively in reference to the theistic argument.

4. Give the Cartesian position to the effect that the knowledge of God is the presupposition of all knowledge. Comment upon this. Give the specific arguments of the

Divine existence presented by Des Cartes.

5. State and criticise [sic] the Kantian objections to (a) the ontological and (b) the teleological arguments.

6. Give John Stuart Mill's doctrine of cause and show its bearing upon the aetiological argument.

7. What is to be said in reply to those who meet the argument based on the order of the world by the doctrine of chance?

8. How does the doctrine of evolution affect the theistic argument based upon the evidence of design in nature?

9. What is meant by Kant's doctrine of relative finality, and how do you reply to it?

10. State with criticisms the doctrine of immanent finality.

"I pledge my honor as a gentleman, that, during this examination, I have neither given nor received assistance."

# THE THIRTEENTH LETTER

From Stanly at Princeton
6 February 1899

This is another letter from Stanly about his exams, and modern readers can relate to a student's worry about test results, but differences between his era and ours are evinced in Stanly's relation of a charming story about his interaction with a professor.

The professor mentioned, Arnold Guyot Cameron, was a splendid person to have think well of one. Princeton University was "The College of New Jersey" until October 1896 when the name was changed to "Princeton University". It was therefore under the school's earlier name that Professor Cameron's father had been educated and joined the faculty as a professor of Greek and later served as Librarian. Stanly's professor was born in 1864 and was educated entirely at home until he entered The College of New Jersey in 1882. After various teaching posts he received his PhD from The College of New Jersey in 1891, then taught French at Yale before returning to teach at Princeton from 1897 to 1905. Although just about fourteen years older than Stanly, by the time Stanly studied under him Professor Cameron had already earned an enviable reputation as an able editor of important French works. His post teaching career included many years as a

February, 1899

journalist with "The Wall Street Journal".

*Monday 4.40*

*Dear Folks: -*

*I guess you think that my letters are rather scarce these days but exams have been so thick that I haven't had scarcely any time to think much less to write but now I am done and so I have time to write. I have just come from my last examination and I am sorry to say I did worse in it than any. In fact I would be almost afraid of not passing except for the fact that my term grade, (recitation I mean) will pull me through all right. The reason I didn't do better was because I have never had an exam under Prof. Cameron before. Next time I will know how to study. A great many of the questions he asked us were about points in the reading that he had mentioned as we read but I had no idea he would expect us to remember for exams.*

*There isn't any danger of my not getting through because he counts recitation grade two thirds and exams only one. I told him all about why I didn't do better and he said he was sorry. I said something about being afraid I wouldn't pass and he said, "No -- Oh No! Mr Roberts Oh No! Your term grade is good, Mr Roberts, very good! <u>Excellent</u> Mr Roberts. You will get through all right" -- so I guess I will.*

*He would pass me on the exam anyway because I got all the translation almost exactly right and some of the other questions too. I got through all my exams all right. On the English one I did fairly well I think. There wasn't any questions except the author names Jane Austin, Hawthorne, Trollope,*

Dickens and we had to write a criticism on a novel of each one.

Saturday came Poetics. I did very well on all except the fourth question. That definition of Aristotles was a big long one he gave us and no one expected that he wanted us to know it by heart. All the boys were fussing about it and I dont think hardly any of them got it.

History came this morning and I got through it all right. The questions were written on the board. I made a copy of them and when I copy them over then I will send them to you next letter.

I don't know what the numbers on the french author examination paper I sent you meant. I didn't put them there. I hope I beat 50 in Const[itution] Law -- That was the paper the figures were on wasn't it?

The letter written Tuesday and Wednesday night was received this morning -- I think that is a very good plan to write that way. I got a whole lot of letters this morning. One from Al Hardie, Craig and Jim Stinson. Al told me to be sure and give you his regards when I wrote.

Craig was rejoicing at having finished all his exams and having PASSED as he wrote it in his letter, in all of them. I have bought me a fountain pen. Am writing with it now. It cost me $2.50 but I thought it was worth it as it is a good one.

I wanted it to take my notes with next term. When you take them with a lead pencil they smear and rub out and are hard to read at night. -- Nearly all the boys use them. I am sorry I didn't have one at the first of the year.

February, 1899

What history is it you are going to study in your class? You may have told me but I have forgotten.

I'll send you some more Princetonians in a day or two. They aren't issued during the exams. I have intended to send them all along but I am seldom down by the P.O. and I never can mail them without going down there. -- However I will turn over a new leaf and try and send them regular after this.

There isn't any particular hurry about the check -- I don't think.

It has been snowing here off and on for several days and it is two or three inches deep now. The thermometer is 28 above and it is fine sleighing. The sleigh bells are jingling all the time.

I was very much interested in the sales. The store certainly must be doing a big business. That was over $9000. gain on the same month as last year. -- I just looked out the window and see it has begun to snow again. If it keeps this up much longer we <u>will</u> <u>have</u> a [big] snow sure enough. We have had a lot of bad weather in the last two or three weeks. In fact, we haven't had any good weather at all. I don't know how I am going to get an envelope big enough to hold this letter and put the questions in and I guess I had better stop before it gets any bigger.

Give my regards to everybody. Tell Charlie Helloa.

Goodbye -- with lots of love --

Stanly

POETICS
February 4, 1899.


1. What is meant by the "art impulse" and what are the conditions requisite for its activity?

2. Are "form" and "significance" in any way opposed to each other?

3. Write a criticism of the following poems:

    a.  THE SICK ROSE
O Rose, thou art sick
The invisible worm
That flies in the night
In the howling storm
Has found out thy bed
Of crimson joy
And his dark secret love
Does life destroy.

    b.  HOME, IN WAR-TIME
She turned the fair page with her fairer
    hand --
More fair and frail than it was wont to
    be;
O'er each remembered thing he loved to
    see
She lingered, and as with a fairy wand
Enchanted it to order. Oft she fanned
New moths unto the sun; and as a bee
Sings through a brake of bells, so
    murmured she.
And so her patient love did understand
The reliquary room. Upon the sill
She fed his favorite bird. "Ah, Robin,
    sing!
He loved thee!" Then she touches a
    sweet string
Of soft recall, and towards the Eastern

*February, 1899*

>     hill
> Smiles all her soul -- for him who cannot hear
> The raven croaking at his carrion ear.

4. State Aristotle's definition of tragedy, and some of the varying interpretations of his meaning.

5. Discuss the importance of Edmund and the Fool in the dramatic structure of <u>King Lear</u>.

"I pledge my honor as a gentleman, that, during this examination, I have neither given nor received assistance."

**THE FOURTEENTH LETTER**

From C.N. in Sherman
14 February 1899

Mailed in a cream enveloped pre-printed with the words "Roberts, Sanford & Taylor Co., Wholesale Hardware Sherman Texas", this letter from C.N. covers two pages of thick cream paper in his neat handwriting.

For those interested in the history of the C.S. Roberts House there is fascinating information here on the heating of the house and its water systems. It must be remembered that when this letter was written our old historic house museum was less than three years old. In the hundred plus years since the mansion was built some things have, of course, been altered in the house, but many things remain the same.

The plumbing, for example, is still rather odd. Also still in the kitchen is the speaking tube by which Charlie "whistled" up to the master bedroom; the tube connected the kitchen and the master bedroom. To gain the attention of a person at the opposite end, one would whistle in the hole at the outlet of the tube. When both parties were in position, each could lift a small lever at the side and the tube would be open at both ends for the participants to speak and to hear. With either "door" closed, however, there was privacy at both ends.

One change which has been made to the house since this letter was written was the removal of the outdoor porch sink. When the home was built a large stone sink was installed to run through the wall between the butler's pantry behind the kitchen and the back of the large porch which surrounded three sides of the house. Since the family often dined on the back porch in the summer, the sink provided an easy way to load dirty dishes back into the house at the place where they would be washed and stored.

Little Leska would have been only thirteen years old when this letter was written and so was not yet, of course, of special interest to Stanly, but it is her father's business which C.N. mentioned as having had so much water damage.

*Sherman Tex*
*Feby 14/99*

*My Dear Boy*

*To day, what is left of it, now 9 oclk PM is St. Valentines Day, and it has occurred to me I will surprise you with, not a Valentine, but a letter in which you may take as much pleasure.*

*We have had in the last week a real freak in the weather unprecedented in this climate. It commenced early in the week to turn cold -- one Norther following another until Friday we had a stiff one. Saturday morning Signal Service said there was a Blizzard bound for Texas -- and the Temperature would fall 20 degrees, it was then about 20 degrees above zero. We hooted at* the idea of it -- about 3 oclk Sat afternoon I was in my office most of the afternoon -- the boys would come back saying it was turning cold fast, about time I started home it was about 6 degrees above zero. I came home & by dark it was 4 above. Our preacher from Denton was at our house, he was not able to get warm. I went to work on water works, shut off the water to stove as soon as we could do it do without it -- by 9 oclk it was about 2 deg below zero -- by 11 oclk 8 below all above was in the corner at the door on back Porch. I then went up in your room got your thermometer & hung it on the South End Porch -- in no time it went to 12 deg below zero -- We all went to bed leaving big fire in Furnace & Kitchen Range --- 3 oclk I got up went down & replenished both fires -- about half past 6, Charley came down whistles up that he could not get the water to run in the kitchen -- he built up the fire & soon whistled up that it was all right. I got up and went down to Thermometer it was 10 below in Corner & 14 [below] on South porch -- the wind was just right to shave you.

 Mama wrote you about our going to S.S. & Church. Had no S.S. & church service in Mr. Parks room -- and had no service at night. I work with our Pipes and other things all afternoon nearly feeling quite sure they would all go up Sunday night – it was just about as cold as Saturday night. Monday we all got up to the store late & tales of woe commenced coming in from all over town. Pipes bursted. Ours at home as far as I then knew, were all right, the upstairs was cut off nothing but kitchen open -- in the middle of the day I turned on upstairs pipes and they wouldnt run -- I shut them off again, until this morning I tried them again -- the cold water ran but the hot water would not. I left them turned on however and this afternoon about 3 or 4 oclk the hot water pipes threw out more or less mud or sand & went to running -- and as far as I can tell everything was all right.

February, 1899

    I confess that I am almost at sea to understand the "modus operenda" of the water connection in my house -- where all the mud or sand or both came from, that came out of the Pipes -- and to night --- sometime after I had let the water, both cold and hot, run in my bathroom I went down on back Porch, and such another mess as I found there, the Wash Place in Corner Porch where the water had been cut off for two months had spewed out several Gallons of muddy water and it had run out on Porch -- where it came from is a mystery to me.

    Well to night the mercury is at 40 degrees above zero -- and after such a spell as we have had, feels really warm -- We buried Mrs R. E. Smith this afternoon 3 oclk. Dr. Moon & Bishop Key officiated. Pall bearers J. D. Joiner, Tom Randolph, Nat Birge, Geo Nordwake, Judge Wilkins Judge Hewl, Mr Wandelaker & myself -- a large Progression. She was buried from their home on Gray's Hill -- Mama & Mrs Moon sat up last night with the Corpse and Mama did not go to the funeral.

    This afternoon about 5 oclk the 4in stand pipe running up in the 3rd story of Murphy's building bursted, or at least, the fire Plug flew out, and soon the water was running down all over the floor in second story, the lawyers office Dr Stephens office & c and then down on through flooding nearly all Murphy's stock on lower floor -- oh such a mess, the clerks were doing their best, with water pouring down on them to protect with Oil Cloth & c the shelves of goods -- I dont know what the damage will be, but I should not think less than 5000.$-- I will call up Judge Galloway in the morning and find out about his damage. I presume his office was well soaked.

    Karne Weems has a baby girl at his house -- born Monday

morning. He was at work today -- the boys are free with their congratulations -- for two or three days business has been sorter at a standstill -- we look for big trade again in a few days. We all hope we will have no more such blizzards, this country is not prepared for them.

Ely & Cook moved out of their old stand to day -- up where the arcade was in Ling Block -- one door above McKinstry & Kimborough's Drug Store. The new Bank from Kansas City is going into the Ely & Cook Corner. I understand the bank has rented it for ten years. Good thing for George Hardwicke. The bank is going to make some changes in the front -- going to put Door in the corner and make some other changes -- you must not mention it in writing back home -- but I would not be surprised if Sanford was not a good deal interested in getting the bank here, the man who is the prime mover in the matter and who will furnish most of the money I understand is a friend of S-- think married some of his wife's relatives. He has been very active in the matter of being interested in who the Bank Atty's and some other officials. He has not been very communicative however. I am quite curious to watch developments and see who will form the Board of Directors & officers in the Bank -- I am satisfied they will make money. Another Bank with right kind of management cant help it. I understand Bay Mill will start up right away -- Dallas Cotton Mill parties will be the main portion operating it. Mr Eubanks, Chilt Andrews and perhaps two or three more Sherman people are interested. We are all so glad to have it start up -- I think we stand a good chance to get a good deal work out of it. I believe I wrote you we were putting a new Galv Iron roof on the Oil Mill -- the weather has been so bad that we have not done anything on it for two weeks or more -- when the weather gets good, it will take a week or more to finish up.

*February, 1899*

    *Joe Etter has been doing all the billing for more than two weeks. Ludlow & Parks got so far behind on their books that I had to relieve Parks of the billing and have Ludlow divide up his work with him -- .*

    *John had such a bad finger for awhile that he could not do much -- he is all right again now -- I think Joe rather likes the billing -- and he does finely -- Copes was sick yesterday and part of today with Grippe, he was out this evening.*

    *Mama says tell you I missed sending you some papers that she told me yesterday to send, they are old now & wont send them -- they were about storms & c --  I tell her you will hear enough about it anyway --*

    *Well I feel quite Grippe myself tonight, have taken about 8 grs of Quinine since I commenced this letter, so I will have to quite and go to bed, now 11 oclk. Thermometer in your room where I am writing 70 deg. Mama is sound asleep in your bed where she has been resting all the day since 10 oclk this morning.*

    *Good-bye -- hope you will find some little interest in my letter. All boys speak of you often & ask about you -- I was up at Bank the other day & Frank Batsell asked me if it was true that you entered Senior Class at Princeton -- he appeared to think it was remarkable -- We all want you to make a good record and believe you will -- Your Papa*

    [In EER's handwriting] *My figures about thermometer are right, Papa forgot --*

## THE FIFTEENTH LETTER

From Stanly at Princeton
27 February 1899

    From years of family letters an engaging portrait of Charlie emerges. Equally capable in kitchen and garden, he was in many ways a treasure as a servant and periodically someone would hire him away from the Roberts family. He was temperamental, however, and either his dissatisfaction with another family or theirs with him would soon land him back with the Roberts. Emma, C.N., and Stanly learned to remain unperturbed during his many departures to work for others and during his long absences due to claims of illness, for they learned he would always return.

    It is probable that the "servant's quarters" behind the Roberts House were built before the present mansion and date from when the smaller Roberts family home on the lot would not have been large enough to house a place for Charlie to rest during the day. At the time Stanly was at Princeton Charlie still maintained his own home off the premises but by the following year, when the Roberts family began their "Grand Tour" in Europe, Charlie moved into the Quarters in order to keep a better eye on the house and grounds in the absence of the owners.

    The detailed letters written to Charlie

from C.N. in Europe bear witness to the fact that the elderly African-American man not only had C.N.'s full trust and confidence in home matters, but in business matters as well. It is also clear from those letters that Charlie must have had a reading vocabulary larger than many of the Caucasian men in town; it is frustrating to not know more about the life and educational background of this man who most probably was born in the South before the abolition of slavery.

About one person mentioned in this letter, however, there is no lack of information: the doings of young Mrs. Cleveland were fully documented in the American press from the time of her White House wedding to the President who had been her guardian. The clipping which Stanly enclosed with his letter is transcribed here.

One other note about the contents of this letter is that special attention should be paid to the date on which Stanly mentioned "Spring" would arrive. Until the 1920's most people counted 1 March as the first Day of Spring, rather than the vernal equinox as we do now. In this tidy fashion of the past, Spring began 1 March, Summer began 1 June, Autumn began 1 September, and Winter began 1 December.

*Monday Aft.*
*1 20 P.M.*

*Dear Folks: --*

Your regular letter was received on time this morning and I will answer it now as I have French at three oclock and Political Economy at five and this will be about my only time to write to day.

Arent the sales for January larger than for any other month before? Seems to me that last January's (1898) were the largest to that time.

I am sorry Charlie has quit but I dont suppose it will be more than a week before he will be back again. If he dont come back you can look around again for a man to do the cooking and also take care of the place.

The weather up here has been very nice until yesterday morning it started to raining and kept it up all day and all night. This morning and this afternoon it is cloudy and dark but not raining -- It looks as if it might begin any moment.

I didnt mean not to go to Conn. in May but go there too. I havent any "objections" to going to Washington and would like to go there only every one tells me that I can see all I would want to see there in one or two days -- I will have a week Easter. It would cost me a good deal to go to Washington and stay a week. I should say $25.00 at least. If I went to Conn it would cost me about $9.00 and that would be the R.R. fare. I dont guess it would be hardly that much -- about $7.50. Then I get my board here ($3.00) for that week refunded -- so it would really cost me

*February, 1899*

but $4.50. I have heard a little about the small-pox in Washington but dont believe it amounts to much. I dont remember ever having been vaccinated. I guess I have however as I can see the place on my arm.

I will go just wherever you all think best Easter and you can let me know.

May says "If you go to Washington instead of coming here, I shall be <u>mad</u> - <u>so there</u>".

It would be fine ["fine" used then as we would say "splendid" now] *for Papa to come to the Hardware Association in June. Then he would be here at our Commencement which comes June 14th.*

Just think -- tomorrow is the last day of Winter -- <u>by the calendar</u> I guess we will have a good deal more Winter here yet.

By the way have you ever opened up the parlor yet -- ? You had three pieces covered didnt you? I <u>bet</u> there isnt a prettier parlor in town than ours.

I will send you a little clipping I cut from a Washington paper about Mrs Cleveland at Princeton.

Dr. Patton preached to us in Chapel yesterday morning. One of his regular <u>philosophical</u> sermons. His text which he mentioned once or twice was, "Seek ye first the kingdom of God and His righteousness and all these things shall be added unto you." Then he made us a short talk at Vesper services at 5 P.M. I didnt go to our class prayer meeting last night as the rain was pouring down.

*Dr. Patton has turned over our Ethics to Prof. Hibben but Prof. Hibben says that he will only lecture until Easter and that then Dr. Patton will take us. I hope he wont for I would rather have Prof. Hibben.*

*Excuse the look of this letter right along here my fountain pen got to throwing ink around rather promiscuously. I guess it needs filling. It always runs too freely when it is nearly empty. I dont think I will ever be satisfied with any other kind of pen after this.*

*Guess I will close this letter before I spill any more ink on it and make it look worse. Goodbye with lots of love to you both.*

*Stanly Roberts*

```
Article: "Mrs Cleveland at Princeton"
```

It is a fact, although the public does not know it, that the member of Mr. Cleveland's household nearest to the hearts of Princetonians is not the ex-President, but his amiable wife. Mr. Cleveland comes to big college affairs, sits on the platform and drives back home in his stately carriage, to remain in retirement until the next occasion of importance.

To the college man Mrs. Cleveland is a sort of patron saint, a goddess or idol in human form. She goes to athletic games with her intimate acquaintances among the professors' wives, and sits in the front row. Sometimes a collegian occupies a position of

*February, 1899*

honor by her side, in which case he is the object of much chaffing at the club that night at dinner.

Mrs. Cleveland lives out of doors at Princeton. In a trap behind a tandem team she drives over every Jersey road within twenty miles, and the country people come out in front of the farm houses to see her pass. She is prominent patroness of college sports, and, armed with a brassey and a niblick, she is a familiar figure on the University golf links. Before the advent of the Clevelands Princeton society existed in hot houses, and its most violent form of athletics was the tea fight. Mrs. Cleveland came, was amused, and played tennis. The colonial dames gazed, ordered fashionable outing skirts and played tennis, too.

Mrs. Cleveland is personally acquainted with most of the upper class men in the University. [Stanly has written in pen after this sentence: This statement isnt so.]

"I met Mrs. Cleveland on the front campus this morning, said a Junior, and she called me by name. Say, but she's a peach!" This is the experience and opinion of a majority of the student body. Mrs. Cleveland will stop sometimes to talk with an under graduate acquaintance on the quadrangle. Then some unfeeling scoundrel will lift his voice and cry out "Yea!" and some one else calls "Heads out!". The unfortunate students' friends stand around at respectful distance and grin, and the student grows red in the face and wishes he were in the tomb of his ancestors or in some equally remote spot. Through it all Mrs. Cleveland wears a look of serious innocence that is perplexing.

### THE SIXTEENTH LETTER

From Emma and C.N. in Sherman
20 March 1899

One can almost picture Emma pausing in her work to write this "stream of consciousness" note. Paragraphing has been added to aid the modern reader but that does unfortunately "lose" the feel of the immediacy of the original letter as her pen (a new one, like Stanly's) flew down the page jotting random bits of news.

As Emma had had to endure so many deaths among her own family and was also always so ready to assist with the care of those less fortunate, health matters were ever a concern to her. The "yellow flags" she mentioned in this letter were the banners which doctors were legally required to place in front of homes where there was an illness considered to be contagious.

C.N. also wrote his part of this letter as an unparagraphed block. His section differed from Emma's in that the bulk of his news was associated with his business. As the letters between the two men immediately previously to this are no longer extant we have to rely on other supporting evidence, such as implications in later letters, to understand the reference to Roberts, Sanford and Taylor employee Will Eubanks.

By 1899, with Taylor dead and Sanford engaged more and more with other business ventures, C.N.'s firm, despite its old name of "Roberts, Sanford and Taylor," was actually owned and managed almost entirely by C.N. Roberts. It seems that this fact was not understood by all the employees and there were some who thought that C.N. did not have the right to make his son a Vice President as soon as Stanly would join the firm.

The letter ends on a lighter note; the reference to "too much Jim" is something which would have brought a knowing smile to the recipient. The town postman was known to be more fond of talking to people than of sorting incoming mail to deliver.

Monday 9<u>15</u> A.M.<br>
March 20, 1899

Dear Sonny Boy,

I have washed the breakfast dishes, made the bed and collected the laundry and clothes. I said I would take things easy this morning as papa and I propose walking out to see Henry and Lula directly after dinner. We have not been there since they came. Purposing and going are two different things. Papa may come to dinner with some insurmountable hinderance.

The South wind is rampant again to day. There was no ice or frost this morning and everything looks springlike, fruit trees blooming, grass and trees getting green. The black birds are also rampant and squawking around in flocks. Yesterday – Sunday was a beautiful day. It was cold enough for a white frost and ice early in the morning, but it became pleasant and springlike, no wind, an ideal Spring day.

Papa was complaining of his head, so I left him in bed and went to S.S. alone. I had a full class, Kate Kerr taught. Kate Brown had just returned from Fort Worth, where she had gone to be with Annie who is sick. You know Annie married and went to Fort Worth to live. Kate left Annie no better and came home that her mother might take her place. She says while she was there, some days there were from twelve to fifteen funerals, principally from meningitis. Annie has typhoid fever. Prof. Case is just back from a little trip he says the yellow flags were flying every where in Dallas.

Clifford will teach the review next week. Dr. Moore gave us a good sermon. The officers nominated, were all elected. There were a few scattering votes for others. When I got home from church I found Papa dressing, he was feeling much better and went with me to teachers meeting.

As soon as I could make some coffee we had dinner. I had nice smothered chicken and cake and bread that I got from Kirtley. I get something from her every week.

Charlie keeps himself very much out of sight. I do not know whether he is doing anything. I do not think he is cooking for any one.

We had a good teachers meeting. Mr. Park lead. I hear very favorable reports of the young people's meeting Kate Grace and Ela Wacker belong to it. They have about twenty members. The Ludlows have not joined it. By the by what about that Aunt of Mr Ludlows? You are making a very poor return if you do not *go to see her and write him about it. Cultivate the good will of all.*

*I am just rich in my new pen. Writing is a pleasure, the only trouble is something interesting to write. This is the fourth letter I have written since I received it on Friday at noon.*

*I am writing on the kitchen table. I hope papa will be able to write a little when he comes at noon. I am anticipating my letter, the one that we get every Monday. I can hardly wait for Jim Stinson to get back. Papa was elected delegate to a S.S.* [Sunday School] *Convention that meets in Waco in April. He thinks he will go -- with lots of love Mamma*

*Dear Boy: Here I am to the surprise of Mama I know, home for Dinner 15 m. before 12, and after dinner we will go out & see Henry & Lula. I dont think Henry is doing anything yet except he may be working with old man Richardson.*

*Everything is quiet at the store this morning. Lane is the only Road man in -- think he is having his teeth worked on today -- Lane does not put in much more time than 4 days a week anyway. He is really the Gentleman of the whole business, indulged to death by his Mother. He really worries me, for he might sell a third more goods than he does if he would get a move on himself, but he is complaining of the La Grippe all the time and has for several months -- all of our goods have advanced and are advancing so fast that we find it extremely difficult to keep up with prices.*

*Sheet iron, Tin Plate, Galv Iron ware in fact everything. Wire & nails were advanced from 50 to 100 & we will make little out of this advance, but not near what we ought to. It is no* trouble at all for our men to go down with prices but they dont know how to go up. Sanford is as bad as any of them. He will complain to me about the boys not doing so & so but let him strike a man from Whitewright -- Gainesville, in fact from anywhere, and he is liable to sell at cost & then tell me that he made 25% -- We ought to make some good money this year, in increased sales & advance in goods altogether. One more month after this will tell the story.

You speak of Will Eubanks, it is understood that when you get ready to come into the house I have the right to say where you will go, and I expect to exercise that right. However I hardly think you will be ready before September. After you get through school, if you study hard & make a good record think it is a good idea for you to rest up a little. When you once get into business the opportunity for rest wont come every year. Well I will have to quit. Mama is about ready to go. We did not get your Monday letter. <u>Too much Jim.</u> I tell Mama we have to excuse you.

Goodbye

PaPa

**THE SEVENTEENTH LETTER**

From Emma in Sherman
31 March 1899


Throughout the correspondence of the family in the 1890s are wonderful glimpses of how the C. S. Roberts House was furnished and used and about what was grown in the garden. Now, when climactic changes have made it difficult to coax old fashioned lilacs to bloom in Sherman, it is startling to remember that a century ago they flourished in the town. Emma loved plants and the garden must have been wonderful during this era.

The house was also filled with plants and flowers. Emma's palms, mentioned in this letter, were the envy of many and, all too often to suit Emma's worry about them, she reluctantly consented to seeing her palms carted away from her home to decorate a church for a wedding or bank a coffin in another home.

A beautiful and well tended garden and many luxuriant houseplants were one of the hallmarks of social standing in the late Victorian period; it is not coincidental that Emma wrote that smelling her bouquet of apple blossoms reminded her to write to her female relatives.

One reason a well tended garden was so

important to the Victorians was that in an era when more people rented homes than owned them, a well tended yard signaled property ownership. Now, when the "Heritage Row Historic District" in which the Roberts House stands is again facing a changing neighborhood with the apartments and rental properties giving way to restored nineteenth century mansions, it is poignant to read how a transition like that was also occurring in the 1890's.

Paragraphing has again been reluctantly added to this brief but newsy letter.

*Friday March 31st, 1899*

*My Dear Son;*

*It is getting late, but I cannot tell what time it is as the clock has stopped. It is quite cloudy and we could hope for rain, but I fear it is too cold for that. I have just finished a letter to Cousin Bet. My Warner Library came this afternoon and I had hard work to tear myself away from it long enough to do my writing. As I did not write in time to have my letter go at noon I will send this one to Princeton. Papa said he would write a short letter and send to East Canaan.*

*We are not through house cleaning, Mrs Kearney and I. We will begin upstairs next week. I had the lower floor in nice order, the parlor open, and palms distributed around in time for the history class yesterday afternoon. We had a slim attendance, sickness, company & c kept many away. Mrs Hazelwood's baby is about to die, that kept several away. Mrs Lee Hasche had* visiting company. Margie telephoned me that she has been sick two days, and that her mother was going to have them all vacinated [sic] that afternoon. We have one case of smallpox in town. It is isolated and there seems to be no danger. It is over towards the Kerrs.

Mary has just brought over my cake and bread and a bunch of lilac. She said Kirtley thought it was going to freeze and so she had thought best to gather it. I think the ink must be getting out of my pen, see what a nice blot I have made. I have been out covering up tender shoots but I doubt its freezing the thermometer is about forty four. The sun is trying to set clear so we will probably get no rain. It has sprinkled several times this afternoon.

The Sturgis house is going up fast. They expect to get in it in May. Mr Murphy bought the two Taylor lots south of Cope's place. I heard that he was going to put up a brick. Our part of town seems to be _the best_. If we could get rid of this Robinson house we would have no houses to rent in the neighborhood. I heard that Mr Robinson was on a trade with former County Superintendent Clayton, for a farm. I do not know how true it is. I think Mr Clayton is dying with consumption and the place would probably be poorly kept up.

I have a vase of apple blossoms near me and they are so pretty and fragrant I must write to Carrie soon and also to Bertha, it is no trouble to write with my new pen. I do not wonder that you feel that you cannot do without having so much writing.

*Lovingly,*

*Mama*

*This letter is rather a scratch. I have written in a hurry.*

**THE EIGHTEENTH LETTER**

From Stanly in Connecticut
30 March 1899

While his parents were delighted that Stanly was getting to know his Father's family in Connecticut, they had encouraged Stanly to visit Washington, D.C. for his Spring break. Stanly, however, chose a visit to his Uncle Ed and wife and Cousin May in East Canaan instead of other travels. As detailed in the Introduction, despite his maturity and adult view of business matters, Stanly was "younger" in many ways than some of the boys in his college class. A visit to relatives held more appeal for him than did the prospect of a week traveling alone. Spring break with his cousin offered Stanly the opportunity for some camaraderie that was probably missing in his Princeton experience.

This letter, like Stanly's on 31 December, was written on his uncle's "East Canaan Company Cooperative Creamery Association" letterhead which bore the name "E. S. Roberts" as Secretary and Treasurer.

*Thursday*

Dear Folks: -

I havent but a little time to write this morning before Clarence will be ready to start to the P.O. and then I will have to give him my letter.

I got here Tuesday night and found all well this time. Uncle Ed was in Hartford but got back yesterday --

We have been having a regular blizzard ever since my arrival. Snow, wind, rain, etc. This [one line at bottom of first page has crumbled away] and all want to know when Mamma is going to have some taken ---

Oh Yes Dr Taylor told me to tell Papa that he would like to have one of those pictures -- I showed him my two and he wanted to take one of them but I told him only one was mine.

It seemed real natural to be back up here again. May and I washed the dishes again last night -- not because we <u>had</u> to this time however.

I came up from New York a different way this time from the one I came before. Last time [one line has crumbled away at bottom of the page] New York, New Haven, & Hartford. Up through the Housatonic valley. I like the latter way the best -- I will go back the same way. Good reason why -- I bought a round trip ticket. I got a letter from Jim yesterday. In fact I have received one from him every day for the last four. He said he had been down to see you all. I guess I will get a letter *from you all about to morrow morning. I havent got time to write more now. Will try again soon. With lots of love --*

*Stanly*

## THE NINETEENTH LETTER

From Stanly in Connecticut
3 April 1899

Although it seems clear that C.N. was hoping to be able to brag about his son's success at Princeton, if Stanly could have gotten into the first group in just one class his parents must have been most pleased it was in Theism.

Stanly's comments in this letter about his clothes remind us that even wealthy young men had far fewer clothes one hundred years ago than now, but they dressed well for class.

Conscious that his parents thought they were giving him a wonderful gift in sending him to Princeton for a year, Stanly, always a thoughtful son, complained very little in his letters of 1898-99 of how unhappy he was at Princeton. Scholastically, his interest lay much more in mathematics and business practices than in the literature, history and philosophy courses he was taking to please his parents. Socially, as detailed in the Introduction, he had a hard time at the college, especially as he had been used to being the center of a crowd of friends at home. Stanly, away from his friends, his girlfriend, his home, his family, and his church and frustrated at the delay in

April, 1899

starting in business and hating the winter in the North complained surprisingly little. C.N. and Emma was astute parents, however, and they may have begun to realize the depth of their son's unhappiness when they read the end of this letter.

*April 3rd, 1899*

*Dear Folks: --*

*It is 7 20 Monday morning and I have been up just one hour and twenty minutes I get up at 6 o'clock and we have breakfast at 6 30 every morning. Last night we went to bed at a quarter past nine.*

*Yesterday morning Uncle Ed, Miss Minnie Briggs, May and I went to church,. After church Charlie and Ned and I walked home together. Miley was also over to spend Sunday. He works at Lakeville a place about twelve miles from here. Had a very good sermon by preacher named Langdon --*

*Saturday night May and I took tea over at Mrs. Briggs. I gave her your love and she was very anxious to be remembered to both of you.*

*I wonder what kind of weather you had for Easter Sunday. It snowed here five or six times yesterday. One minute the sun would be shining out brightly and the next a snow squall would come over the mountains and the ground would be getting white. The snow has been on the ground ever since I got here. It has looked a great deal more like January weather than either March or April weather. There is ever so much difference between* here and Princeton.  It is ever so much warmer there.

I have a new suit waiting there for me when I get back --- you know that black suit I have with the _frock_ (swallowtail) coat. I think I will buy me a coat to go with that suit and wear it for every day -- This is a good suit [coat]  but I cant wear it with that suit.

By this time you have gotten my report. What do you think of it. I think it is very good. I got mine since I have been here. I wrote to the office and told them to send it to me. You see I got first group in Theism. The one I was afraid of. I thought I did pretty well in it however.

Ill answer all these questions about Mifflin & Miss McCord etc in my next letter when I get back to Princeton -- I wont have time now as it wont be a but a few minutes before Clarence starts for the office.

My next letter will be from Princeton and I guess I will be feeling rather blue -- I will get back there Thursday night. With lots of love from Uncle Ed, Auntie, May and myself.

Stanly

## THE TWENTIETH LETTER

From Emma and C.N. in
Sherman 6 April 1899

Education and reading were always very important to Emma, as this letter gives ample proof. One of C.N.'s wedding gifts to Emma had been a complete set of Dickens' books. C.N. was also fond of reading but in the family it was Emma who was considered "the scholar". It is an interesting peek into the marital financial habits of one hundred years ago to learn that Emma had use of her own money to put towards the purchase of a set of expensive books.

In this letter C.N. touched on the national concern about "Trusts" which was of particular worry at the time to many Americans and particularly to businessmen like himself. C.N. also wrote to his son about an issue that would stir passions in Stanly -- a proposed name change for Stanly's first college. Periodically in its early history there were discussions as to whether "Austin College" should change its name, since it was nowhere near Austin, the state capitol. Despite several name change attempts, "Austin College" continues today as a small liberal arts college in Sherman, Texas -- 200 miles north of the town of Austin. "Princeton University", of course, was still considered a new name as the institution had been "The College of New Jersey" until just a few years pervious to Stanly's year there.

*Thursday 3<u>35</u> P.M.*
*April 6th, 1899*

*Dear Sonny,*

*Papa brought your letter at noon, the last one we will get from Canaan. This is the day for your return to Princeton and if it looks as gloomy there as it does here it will not enliven your spirits.*

*We are having our first rain in a long time and it is very grateful to us. Yesterday morning the first drops came but it amounted to very little yesterday, did not keep me from attending the benevolent society. It has done a little better to day. We have had a <u>very</u> gentle rain most of the day. The wind is in the north and there is some danger of a freeze to night. The thermometer is about 45. I would be very sorry to see my roses freeze but it would be quite an undertaking to get out there in the mud and cover them all up it is not raining now but looks dark and threatening.*

*I was all through housecleaning but a half days work, that will have to wait for fair weather. All except what I want Mr. Knolls to do in the cellar and on the porches. I have him wipe off the weather boarding on the porches. He came several days ago but then it was too dusty now it is too damp. Next week he will have to go to McKinney in his R.R. case, so I do not know when I can have it done unless it clears up in time this week.*

*April, 1899*

*I wrote you that my Warner books -- Library -- had come. We got your little revolving bookcase out of the attic, took the legs off, so that it sets flat on the floor, and polished it up. We put in three shelves and the books fit nicely, one side, of course, just as though it was made for the purpose. It looks very nice indeed. But sometime I hope to have another case with sliding doors just like the other one. I like to have the books under glass. I had Mrs. Kearny clean up the attic. It was so dusty I hated to go up there.*

*Last night I was reading one of my Warner Library -- enjoying it so much -- and reading bits out to Papa, when he said "When Stanly comes home I wish he would commence, and keep up, a course of good reading, and <u>store his memory</u>. I do not want him to never have a thought above drudgery." What did the Britanica* [sic] *cost? The "W.L." is $.90 four and a half off for cash payment. We have paid it out, I paid $55. and Papa $30.50.*

*I did not go to prayer meeting last night. I felt tired after my house cleaning and I had already been up to the Benevolent Society. Papa would have gone to Presbytery at Dallas to day if it had not been for leaving me alone. I could have gotten Grace to stay with me at night, but I could not have very well attended to the furnace and I would have been very lonesome by myself all the three days. We still need to have fires a good part of the time. I suppose as long as they continue to have snow storms -- even in Mo -- we cannot expect very warm weather. We certainly have had fires for a long time. You remember we had a cold spell before you went off. I wrote you how pleased we were with your report. Papa says Dr. Sampson thought it was fine. I will get Papa to write some to night to go in this letter.*

With much love,

Mamma


My Dear Boy: I brought home my Book to night to get off some remittances for tomorrow but Mama always wants me to write some for her letter so I expect my remittances will go by default.

Weather has been such that we have not had much business this week, but if we can only have several days rain & not too cold we can well afford to do nothing for the Farmers need the rain.

We bought to day three cars Iron -- 1 each Corrugated -- Galvanized & Block -- this makes seven cars sheet iron we have bought in last 15 or 20 days. We have bought 60 cars goods I recon [sic] within past four or five weeks, and yet have to buy several more. Everything has gone into the hands of trusts and is going. I am afraid they will ruin our country. It makes me <u>dizzy</u> to read of their organizing. The idea that the Government can do anything with them is absurd -- they will control the Government.

I saw Dr Sampson yesterday he was right hot at Butte for his action in the matter of changing the name of Austin College. He wrote a circular letter to all of the Trustees and perhaps to all the "Alumni" of A.C. charging Dr S with taking the advantage of the Alumni & c. He sent me one of the letters. Butte is an upstart. You know they elected him a trustee last meeting of the Synod and it spoiled him. Sampson will <u>lay</u> <u>him</u> <u>out</u>  [This expression meant that Dr. Sampson would show other people what Butte was really like.]

though, he showed me a letter I think he will send to some of the church papers, explaining his position as to change of Austin College name -- & c -- and he took occasion to blister Mr. Butte. I believe he will demand the resignation of Mr B at the next meeting of the Board -- in June.

I closed the trade yesterday with French & Carlton to paint the college, and also ordered the fence for the Campus a few days ago. We expect to have all the work done before the next Commencement. You know it is going to be the "Semi Centennial" for the College. They expect to have a great time. Dr. Sampson is making or has made considerable preparation.

You will hardly know the place when you come back. Mrs Ball of Kingston recently gave the College $5000. and this is helping make above improvements.

Prof Bell came in to see me a day or two ago, asked a good deal about you -- I told him about your report he did not appear to be surprised he said that he knew you would make a good record, he appears to regret that you did not take Greek here & then a full A.B. & A.M. course at Princeton --

Dr. Moore told me a day or two since that he wanted John to go to Princeton one year anyway, when he gets through here -- He thinks John is making better record at the college this year then he has ever made before.

John Williams and Mrs. Irwin are in Dallas this week as delegates to the Sunday School Convention. Went down yesterday. He told me he was going to stay and attend Presbytery, it meets there to day, Mrs Verison went down as our Delegate this morning, and I think Dr Moore went down this afternoon --

*Mamma says for you to get the Coat as you said & wear your suit -- she neglected to write you so --*

*We suppose you saw Dr Taylor both going & coming. You ought to be pretty well acquainted in New York. When you go back to New England in June, I want you to go around & see the factories. I can send you a letter that will introduce you to a great many of them.*

*Well it is 10 oclock and I have been sleepy all the afternoon so I must quit & go to bed. Mama wants to have me read her what I have written you. I am almost afraid to do it for fear I will want to tear it up & not send it.*

*Mama is loud in praise of the Fountain Pen. I filled it for her at Dinner. Well, we hope you are not homesick to night and feel refreshed and ready to take good hold of your studies again -- remember you have only a few weeks more to do all you will ever do at Princeton -- hope you will think of the time as precious. Good bye & good night -- with much love from MaMa & -- PaPa--*

## THE TWENTY FIRST LETTER

From Stanly at Princeton 7
April 1899

We know very little about the war years in C.N.'s life, just that he wished to serve in the Confederacy but that he requested a commissary position so as not to meet his Federal brothers on the battlefield. At least one other of the six Roberts brothers also supported the Confederate cause. Much has been written about Maryland as a troubled border state with "split" families but the Roberts' home state of Connecticut also had families with divided loyalties. The Roberts' family spilt seems to have healed remarkably quickly after the war, since one of the brothers who supported the North joined C.N. and another "Confederate" brother in the South immediately after the war. However, it would be following a typical pattern if residents of C.N.'s home town were not so quick to forget C.N.'s support of an opposing side in a war. Perhaps that is why Stanly made much of the fact that while in Connecticut he had heard kind inquiries and comments about C.N.

Another lapse in our knowledge of Roberts family history is that we know nothing about Stanly's girlfriend in Coleman except what was revealed in this and a later letter in this collection. Despite how Stanly may have felt about her at the time of these letters, she was not destined to be his bride, for Stanly was single and quite heart-whole when he fell in love with Leska Murphy about six years later. Their sixty-five years of "happily ever after" anniversary cards to each other read like the conclusion of fairy tales. In fact, they celebrated their anniversary not once a year but once a <u>month</u>.

    The fellow classmates which Stanly mentioned in this letter are believed to have been members of the same eating club to which Stanly belonged. Although Stanly took many of his meals at his boarding house, he did belong to an eating club; eating clubs were the equivalent of fraternities at Princeton. In the absence of dormitory mates, fellow eating club members would have been expected to be Stanly's closest friends at the school. In order for his parents to not realize how solitary a figure he was at the campus, in a letter now missing Stanly may have lead his parents to believe he was close to the men with whom he occasionally ate. In this letter Stanly responded to questions about the class standing of some of the students whom his parents thought were friends of his. Test standings were posted publicly so Stanly was able to answer even though he may not have discussed the matter with the students mentioned.

April, 1899

*Princeton, N.J--*
*Friday -- 2-20 P.M.*

Dear Folks: --

Well I am back in Princeton, again and I guess my vacations are over until June. It comes very near giving me the blues when I think that I have two months before me with nothing whatever to do but just study study study. There will be absolutely nothing else to do except a few baseball games to go to. If the time will only go as fast however as it did before Easter it wont seem so very long before June.

I didnt get back from Conn. until last night. I would have come back Tuesday but as I only had two classes Wednesday and only one Thursday and all easy I decided to stay over. I left Conn. yesterday morning at 8.A.M. and got into N.Y. at 11_30_ A.M. Went up to Dr Taylor's office and he told me that Court was down at his room and was going off on the 3_30_ train. I went down but Court had just gone out -- and so I did not get to see him. I wandered around the city awhile went to Siegel Coopers & bought some music for May and then about five o'clock went back to Dr Taylors office. We went down to his rooms and then out to dinner (supper).

I left him at the table for I had to hurry to catch my boat which left Courtland St at 7_50_. Left Jersey City at 8_02_ and got here to Princeton at 9_23_.

Wednesday night I went to a sugar party. It was at East Caanan in a little hall about thirty feet square. All of us went -- Auntie, Uncle Ed, Miss Minnie Briggs (or Auntie Deliverance as May and I call her) May and myself. They had a phonographic entertainment first and then we went down stairs and had maple syrup and maple sugar to eat -- with hot bread etc. Then they moved the benches away up stairs and had a regular old fashioned country dance. I told May it looked like to me too hard work for so little fun. I saw a man dancing that must have been over sixty.

Mr Briggs, Aunties brother, came up and introduced himself to me and then his wife. He said all kinds of nice things about Papa and went on to say how sorry he was that he didnt see me when I was there Christmas.

He and everybody else I saw up there said they hoped you could both come up in June. They all asked me it you were coming.

I am glad you liked my report. I thought it was pretty good myself. I dont think I stand much chance for prizes -- There are scarcely any given except in connection with Essay writing and I never could write much of an essay.

I am very much interested in all Papa writes about the store. I think myself that probably the very best place for me would be in the front of the Retail. What salary do you suppose I would start in on. I received the picture of the store this morning with the picture of the Cleveland man in front. Two or three of the boys here who saw it said they had seen the Cleveland agent before. Cape & John & Arthur all looked very natural in the front door and I think I discovered Mr Ludlow back of the window.

I havent seen Mifflin since I came back. I saw him just before I left. He said they were all going to leave for Europe early in June, even before college is out. They are going to Turkey, Greece, Russia and everywhere else.

*April, 1899*

 *Mamma asked me in one letter if I was still writing to a certain Texas girl as often as ever. I guess I am and one thing I want to do this summer instead of staying up north so long is to come home and then go out to Coleman to see her.* <u>*Can I?*</u>

 *It is raining here now. I wish you could have some of the rain we are having. It rains here nearly all the time. I saw in the paper however where it had been raining in Northern Texas so I guess you are having your share now.*

 *I dont know what Group Quackenbush got. Havent seen him since Easter. Dont think he's back yet.*

 *Williams got 2nd Group too; he is good. He got 1st Group in Bible also. Smith got 4th Group. He studies real hard but he failed in chemistry and that pulled him down.*

 *I found my new suit of clothes at the express office when I got back. It fits all right and I like it real well. I dont expect to wear it much at least not for some time to come. I am still wearing my heavy winter clothes and they are very comfortable.*

 *I must stop now. With lots of love to you both.*

 *All the Conn. folks asked to be remembered and sent love -*

 *Stanly --*

**THE TWENTY SECOND LETTER**

From Stanly at Princeton
10 April 1899

The "wheel" to which Stanly referred in this letter was, of course, his bicycle. With his enthusiasm for bicycles, Stanly was part of the most popular fad of his era. The invention of the pneumatic wheel in 1889 had made bicycle riding so comfortable that yearly sales almost doubled each year for the next decade until reaching an all time high of 1.2 million bicycles sold in 1899.

Some communities considered the bicycle riding men a danger to their streets and many towns tried to enforce ordinances about speed and hours of riding. In response, bicyclists formed the League of American Wheelmen and agitated for better roads. Before the end of another decade, however, young men were more interested in cars than in bicycles; in 1909 only 160,000 bicycles were sold. Of course, many of those 1909 sales were to woman and a whole new set of societal concerns and freedoms were born.

April, 1899

*Monday -- 4<u>15</u> P.M.*

Dear Folks: --

I have just three quarters of an hour in which to write. You know Monday is my busy day. I have just got back from French and at five comes Political Economy. You asked me about Mifflin. I havent seen him since I got back -- I got a letter from Mabel the other day, the first I have received in a long while -- Your letters received at usual time this morning and very much enjoyed.

It is bright and pretty here today -- Thermometer 47--

Grass green and trees are budding -- and things are spring like indeed. It begins to look now like we might have a good deal of pretty weather -- It has rained here so much.

I took my wheel down to a shop here and had them give it a thorough over hauling -- cleaning and repairing etc. It was in rather bad shape. Cost me $2.00 to have it all fixed up. It isnt like having Jim do it and paying for the time he takes --

The Britannic cost $84.00. You said the Warner Library cost $.90. I should think it was a rather cheap lot of books if the whole things only cost 90 cents. What is the Warner Library --? Is it fiction or what?

I got one of the letters from Geo Butte about the change of the name of the college. His objections to the change of the name of the College is that it will be bad for the old Alumni. People will ask them where they graduated and when they say Austin College they wont know what college they mean. People do get mixed up with the University however.

I dont think half of the Professors here who voted to allow my entrance to the Senior Class ever got it into their head straight that I was from <u>Austin College</u> and not from the U. of T. at Austin Texas.

Does Dr. Moore mean that he is going to send John to Princeton this next year -- If he does intend to and will let me know I could very probably help him a good deal in seeing about a room etc.

I don't think he could get in a dormitory and in fact I think he would like it better to get a room in town like mine. He <u>might</u> be able to get mine if he wanted it.

Yes I saw Dr Taylor both going & coming but only a few hours each time. I <u>am</u> pretty well acquainted with New York. Can go all over it without the least trouble and know where almost everything in the City of any importance is. Just what streets the Waldorf Astoria, Hoffman House, etc are -- etc etc etc.

Just five more weeks (counting this one) of regular work. Then our exams begin. They begin May 15th & close May 27th.

I am going to buy that coat and also a pair of bicycle pants. I had a heavy winter pair but I knew I would not need them anymore so I sold them to a fellow. I am going to buy me a light pair for spring. I wear out my other pants so soon riding a wheel. When I get the coat and pants I will have all the clothes I will need for some time.

Mamma asked me if I met any of the girls here. Well I

should say not. I havent been to call on a girl since I left home. If it wasnt for eating with the crowd I do I dont suppose I would speak to any female besides my landlady more than once in six months.

It is getting most time for Polit. Econ. Class and so I will have to bring this very interesting (?) letter to a close.

With lots of love

Stanly --

## THE TWENTY THIRD LETTER

From Emma and C.N. in Sherman
13 April 1899

Like many devout conservative Christians, Emma and C.N. did not care to use the word "revival" since the term was seen to presuppose private, internal beliefs. Instead, they made use of the term "protracted service" to describe a series of religious services which were held with a view of increasing church membership and renewing the commitment of those who were already church members.

Emma eschewed anything showy in her words or manner. As explained in the Introduction, she wore only black or very dark colors and she wore no jewelry. She admired pretty clothes and decorative items on others and her decision to equate drab attire with spiritual piety was one she made for herself alone. Her private religious writings make it clear that she did not believe "harmless frivolity" of any kind was wrong for people who did not feel "called", as she did, to dress plainly. It was in keeping with this modest approach to life for herself which caused Emma to be hesitant about having her picture taken. There are, in fact, very few photographs of Emma extant.

The history work to which she referred

April, 1899

was for her monthly study group.

*Thursday 11 30 A.M.*
*April 13th, 1899*

*Dear Sonny,*

*I have dinner underway, and am sitting at the kitchen table. Outside, the south wind is blowing things at will. Though it is a very backward Spring, things are looking quite green and Springlike, even the pecan and walnuts are putting out. The drouth continues and things are slow on that account.*

*We had a fine prayer meeting last night. S.S. room good half full. Quite a number of young people out. Prof. Thompson asked the members of the Y. P. S.* [Young People's Society] *to remain after prayer meeting, and there were quite a number. Dr. Moore expects to begin a protracted service the latter part of April. Mr. Pierson is visiting Mr. Smith. He will preach for us on Sunday if he remains over. I think Dr. Moore hopes to have him begin the continued service and then he expects to get Mr. French from Fort Worth.*

*Last night John Williams asked me if it was true that you had the Salutatory at Princeton. He said he had heard of you writing some thing of the kind to Mary Sampson. Prof. Thompson asked Capt. Roberts the same question. Papa took your report and one of the Princetonians up this morning to show Prof. Thompson. Kirtley spent most of yesterday afternoon with me. I read her your last letter. She said it was a good letter. I admire Jannette Sampson more than many. She has quite a sweet face. I am only judging the outside, I know them so slightly.*

*Just think, next month will be May, and then next month will be June! I am sure it will pass very rapidly if you study hard, and you will want to put in your best <u>licks</u> since so many are interested in your success. We have told several that you said you would know better how to prepare for another examination. Will you be classed at the last one? Don't leave all the studying to do at the last. I do not like to think of you looking so sleepy.*

*I am thinking of having my picture taken, perhaps you will get one by and bay.*

*3<u>45</u> P.M. Papa came to dinner and so postponed the writing. I told him if he would wait for me I would go up with him and have my picture taken. He consented, and so I have been and gone and done it! I have no idea how they will look. I am sorry I did not have them taken when it was cool enough to wear my winter dress, as I think it would have looked better. I then went up to Dr. Gunby's office and had him pierce the place on my eye with an electric needle. He says I may have to come back once more.*

*I told Papa he could tell Charlie that if he wants to cook again he could come back the first of May. He is very much spoiled though, has gotten some good jobs. Says he does not know that he wants to cook. Can make more money without. That we do not pay him enough &. c. He got paid extra well for some work that he did at Mrs. Birges and that has spoiled him. She gives some entertainment this after noon. Papa conveyed a wrong impression, Charlie thinks he can come back any time until the first of May. I meant he could not come back until the first of May. He did not get that impression at all. I certainly will not pay him any more. And I suppose he would be more independent* than ever if he should come back, which Papa thinks he has no idea of doing.

Joe said he supposed I was "proud of you", when I was at the store this afternoon. Papa brought your letter at noon. Thermometer here is nearly 80. One hot day a week or so ago it was up to 90, or over, and the next day it was quite cold.

I think I remember, since you mention it that I put the decimal on the wrong side. The "Warner Library" is a collection of the world's best literature. There are thirty volumes and they cost $90.

Just getting the report from your other examination makes the next one seem to come soon. In the report they count conduct, absence and everything. I am afraid you are going to pull down your next examination with the latter. You were off with Jim and then staid over time in Conn. Try and not miss another single time. Dr. Moore <u>wants</u> to send John to Princeton next year, but I suppose it is not at all certain. I feel sure he will want him to go as economically as possible. I do not think he would pay what you do for board. You can prepare yourself to give him information when you return.

What did Mabel write? Did she say anything about their trip? I did not answer Mrs. Hard's letter, received some time ago. I felt like she would not care to keep exchanging notes, and that was all hers amounted to. And I made no reply when she sent me the paper about Gen. Hood except the verbal message through you.

When you answer Mabel's letter, tell them, I wish them a very happy Summer, which I have no doubt they will have. We had a very pleasant time at Mrs. Hardwickes the other afternoon. We worked on Mrs. Cunningham's silk slumber robe. The party was given to Mrs. Cunningham. Mrs. Moore, Mrs. Speake, Mrs. Scott and ladies of that age were present, nearly all Presbyterians. We had nice refreshments. Her house is quite pretty and she had plenty flowers from her green house.

I must close now and give my 'history' a little time, to morrow will be the day, and I have given it very little thought. We meet with Mrs. Shury this week.

With much love

Mamma


Dear Boy: Mama always expects me to write some in closing her letter, but tonight I want to go to the Protracted Service at the Baptist Church so cant write much.

Mama will get her pictures about Monday or Tuesday. She is awfully afraid she will not like them. It was like pulling teeth to have them taken. Except her desire to send one to you, dont believe we would have ever gotten them.

Goodbye,

Papa

## THE TWENTY FOURTH LETTER

From Stanly at Princeton
14 April 1899

This letter gave Stanly's parents a little more information about Stanly's romantic interest at the time of this series of correspondence. Also contained in this letter is more information about Stanly and his entry into his father's business.

*Friday April 14th 3 20 P.M.*

*Dear Folks: -- Its hot -- awful hot -- here today. I mean for this time of year. Thermometer says 80. We have been having beautiful weather for the past week. It is cloudy this afternoon and I think we will have an April shower before night -- I hope so. It will cool things off.*

*I got your letter this morning -- You told me not to write till I had been to see Mr Ludlows Aunt. As I had three classes this A.M. and have a written recitation in Prose French today I am afraid I cant get around there to day -- I will try and go some day next week. I will have to hunt up Mr. Ludolow's letter for I* have forgotten her name --

I am glad you dont object to my going to Coleman this summer. Coleman is out in West Texas just south of Abilene. Shall I write you a young history of Miss McCord --? Here it is -- She is very nearly nineteen years old, rather good looking and I <u>don't</u> think she is a "butterfly". Her Father & mother are old school Presbyterians. Her Father I believe is in the Banking & Real Estate Business. She has three sisters all older than herself, two of whom are married. Two brothers, one of whom went to Austin College for several years. The other is about thirty I think and also in Real estate Business. Her "Educational Qualifications" are very good. She went to Mrs. Keys for nearly two years and somewhere else before that. Now, dont you think I have given an exhaustive history?

Mifflin was over a little while yesterday afternoon. I dont see him quite as often as I use to do --

Every night now just after supper the Seniors get out on the steps in front of Nassau Hall and sing. It sounds real pretty! Guess I well go back to Conn again about the 27th of May. Our exams end then -- Then I have to be back here again about the 12th to 14th for Graduation.

About the business. I think you (Papa) will be the best judge of the place I ought to take -- I want to be where I will do the most good -- for the business and also where I can get on the best -- Would I be able to get along as fast in Keenes place as I would in the retail?

What make[s] prices all so demoralized?

*April, 1899*

*Are you going to take stock the first of May? I got a second letter from George Butte this morning asking me to give my opinion in regard to the change of name of the College. He said that you wrote him saying "I seriously doubt the propriety of a change" Did you mean change of the Boards action or change of name. I hate to see the name changed because it will make the alumnus of a college with a different name. There is some consolation however in being a graduate of Princeton.*

*I am wearing short pants again now all the time. Bought me a pair of gray Golf pants. It saves my others and then its nice to run downstairs jump on my wheel and be off without bothering about pants guards etc.*

*When I get back to Sherman I think I will wear them there and if people dont like it I dont know what they will do. I am taking it easy while writing this letter. I am laying flat on my back on the bed with my paper on a book propped up by the knee in front of me. Another advantage of a fountain pen -- Its getting rather late and so I will say goodbye for this time. With lots of love*

*Stanly*

*Friday -- Apr 21 -- 99 -- <u>12. M</u>*

*No wonder you didnt receive my letter in time. While over at Prose Fiction just now I put my hand in my pocket and found my letter which had been reposing there since last Friday -- just one week -- I will send it along any way -- I guess you must think I am <u>lost</u> by this time.*

*I put the letter in my pocket to mail and thought that I had done so --*

*You will have two to read now. Goodbye*

*Stanly*

## THE TWENTY FIFTH LETTER

From Stanly at Princeton
18 April 1899

News of Charlie's work habits occasioned an interesting comment from Stanly, in this letter, about wages.

A reminder that technological advances have cost us as much as they have helped is shown here in the reference to the evening activities of the college boys. Before inexpensive ways to play recorded music dominated college campuses, students often gathered to sing.

*Tuesday Morning*

*Dear Folks: --*

*I am one day late with this letter. Yesterday I had a long French lesson to get out. Hereafter I will be able to write on Monday without any trouble. We had our last French recitation yesterday. From now on until the end of the term we will have a lecture at that hour on Monday.*

*I am so glad that that picture has been taken at last. I am* in hopes that I shall receive one of them by the end of this week. I hope they will be real good. I will have two pictures of both of you on my mantel.

The way I am writing this letter, the order of the pages I mean, is not any new way I have discovered but simply a mistake I made by starting out on the wrong page.

Its funny what ideas people can get into their heads. I dont think I ever mentioned salutatory to Mary. D. Sampson. In fact I am sure I didnt.

A fellow named Shultz is Salutatorian. He has been here four years (as he would have to be to get it) and on the First group every time.

I think when I get back home I will find Charlie back in his same old place in the kitchen. He must be crazy about wages. Some of these colored fellows up here dont get much more than he does and they have thirty five or forty to wait on instead of two.

We are having fine weather here again. Had a little sort of cool spell Sunday. Thermometer went down to 38. Its up between 60 & 70 again now. The warmest we have had it here yet was 82 one day last week.

I havent seen Mifflin for two or three days. I think I will go over to his room this afternoon. I will send you Mabels letter. I havent written to her yet but will just as soon as I have time. I havent been writing to anybody much lately. I got <u>three</u> postal cards from Jim yesterday and all they said was "you owe me three letters" --

*April, 1899*

*Princeton isnt near so dull now as it was a month or two back.*

*I told you didnt I about senior singing? Every evening about dark the Seniors sit on the steps of Old North and sing songs and all the rest of the college and some of the town people come over on the campus in front.*

*Then there is a baseball game every Wednesday and Saturday. I have been to two or three of them*

*I am going tomorrow afternoon. Princeton is to play Lafayette and they say it will be a fine game. It is chapel time so I will have to jump on my wheel and rush over. Will finish when I get back.*

*Chapel is over and I must finish this letter and study Political Economy.*

*I guess the Store will have their hands full in a week or two now taking stock won't they? I saw in some paper where the Texas Legislature passed a law against Trusts. Dont suppose that amounts to much does it?*

*Excuse me for remarking on the weather again but it is just simply <u>glorious</u> this morning. A fellow over at chapel just now said he didnt have but one objection to this weather and that was that he couldn't "pole"* [A period slang for "complain"] *at all.*

*The mail man will be here now in about fifteen minutes but I dont suppose he will bring me any letters this morning unless its one from May --*

*I must stop now and do some studying. Goodbye. With lots of love.*

*Stanly*

## THE TWENTY SIXTH LETTER

From Emma and C.N. in Sherman
18 April 1899

This letter gives another valuable glimpse into the world of the Roberts House one hundred years ago with the news of the garden, daily activities of Emma and Stanly, and business.

The book Emma was reading, "Our Village" was written by Mary Russell Mitford in 1830. This charming classic was reissued many times throughout the nineteenth century. It is likely that Emma was reading the very popular 1893 edition which was brought out with a special introduction by Anne Thackray Ritchie.

In his portion of the letter, C.N. wrote of the "Atwood call on you". Stanly had probably received a letter from a Mr. Atwood, "calling" for funds in the manner which usually accompanied the protracted meetings at this time. Each member was told the amount they should consider giving and asked to specify the uses of those funds. C.N. wrote advising Stanly that he did not need to give to this but if he did, C.N. suggested Foreign Missions as the designee.

Tuesday 10 A.M.
April 18, '99

My Dear Son:

I was somewhat disappointed that I did not receive a letter yesterday. I suppose you did not get yours on time and waited for it. I expected to go up and have another sitting for my picture this morning, but, when I was almost ready quite a blowing rain came up. I have the negatives of the other sitting. I think one of them will work up tolerably well. I do not like the other one at all. Even in the best one the hair is rather blowsy and I do not like the dress, so in the next one I am going to wear my winter dress and have little or no friz about my hair.

I will go this afternoon if the weather will do at all. Mrs. Muse has just telephoned me about a 'case' in this ward that needs looking after, and we will have to try and attend to that also this afternoon. I hardly know what to write you this morning, there is so little of interest occurring. Yesterday morning, I had Mr. Knolls set out my geraniums, oleanders & c and with his assistance I repotted most of my palms and other plants that are to remain in the pots. Then we had him clean out the cellar. He was to have returned this morning had it not rained.

Mrs. Cape Taylor came to see me yesterday with her two babies. She is going home soon to be present at her sister's wedding. She expects to return in June and be here through the summer. Mrs. Taylor and Louise expect to visit in Ill. and also at Eureka. Jim Stinson asked papa yesterday when he had heard from you, said he had not heard from you in three weeks.

Papa remarked to me that he expected, or rather, thought

*that you were studying. Mrs. Speake spent almost the whole of yesterday afternoon with me. Every now and then it lightens up as though it would clear off, and again, looks dark as though it would rain. We have had some rain, but more would be acceptable.*

*I am sorry we have not gotten our grass planted yet. We have been waiting on Mr. McCan and he has never returned to attend to it. I wanted him to do it for I think he will do it better than Mr. Knolls, but it ought to be in now and get the benefit of the April rains. Charlie is on crutches, has rheumatism in one foot. It is so swollen that he cannot bear his weight on it. He told papa that it waked him in the night Friday night, it pained him so.*

*He had a negro man attending to the church and waiting on him Sunday. Papa sent him up the crutches yesterday. I should think it would make him realize he ought to save some money, when he can work. I am reading such a nice little book of sketches called "Our Village" by an English author. One Prof. Morrison lent me. I told Papa to be sure and write some too in this letter.*

*Lovingly, Mamma*

*Dear Boy*

*As usual I am obeying Mamas wish in scribbling something for you. Mama is getting ready to go up town with me. We have just had our dinner. Weather out is warm & partly clear only -- it did not make out to rain much more than to settle the dust, but probably will rain more. Everything at the store is moving off as usual all the Boys in their places -- there will be a good deal of building going on in town this summer -- In the Bay Mill Addition there will be a good many small cottages built. Mr*

Etter is building two. Cope talks about building one -- Lyon & Co will build several -- then I think Mr Murphy will build. A Public School building will be built & c. There is a good deal of building going on in the small towns. I sent Tennille to Whitewright this morning to try to see about some work there and think I will send him to Bonham tomorrow or next day --

 We work five hands in shop most all the time and Jim Roberts and the younger Herndon run the Bicycle Shop. I think Jerry Herndon is Jim's Apprentice. Our Bicycle repair work keeps Jim pretty busy. We are not carrying as much stock in Wheels this year as last, but order as we sell. We keep big stock of Bicycle Supplies & C -- Jo attends to same as usual -- Jo is building him a house -- dont know what he expects it to cost, he told me that he was almost afraid to spend much in a house as he did not know how we were going to come out in the business.

 Our sale for March will out run any month we ever had -- dont know yet, but I think will run up to $30,000.00 perhaps over -- this month of course will be the last for the Fiscal Year -- and we will soon know what we have done -- we are going to have the biggest stock to take that we ever had --

 Well Mamma & I have been up to Snells. She sat for her picture & gone back home, and I am at my desk. Cant write any more as I have several matters to attend to. Snell told us he could not get any of Mamas pictures ready before next Wednesday -- tomorrow week. So it will be several days after that before you get one.

 I rather dread the next, you may say, four weeks work & c -- week after next our state "Hardware Jobbers Association" will meet in Sherman -- We have got to <u>father that</u>, then stock taking

& wind up for the year. At same time commencing with next Sunday, Dr. Moore or rather our church will hold Protracted meeting. Dr. Richardson from McKinney commences it & Dr. French from Fort Worth will continue from the 4th July on --

    As to the Atwood call on you I dont think there is any obligation for you to contribute to that -- if you wanted to give what he asks to anything would give to Foreign Missions.

    Well good bye -- for this time.

    Papa

## THE TWENTY SEVENTH LETTER

From Emma and C.N. in Sherman
20 April 1899

The lives of two content, busy people of 1899 are perfectly conveyed in this letter. Emma wrote of her reading and cooking, of her benevolent society work and of the other minutia of daily life for a middle class wife. C.N. wrote of his own business, of the business world in general, and of the weather. Neither wrote of earth-shaking events but the small details they wrote of were just what Stanly wished to read and, over one hundred years later, they are just what we wish to read, too, in order to understand life in the late nineteenth century. Paragraphing has been added.

*Thursday 11 45 A.M.*
*April 20, '99*

My Dear Son;

We have not received a letter from you this week. I think it was to day a week ago that we received the last. Such a thing has not occurred before since you left. We think one letter must

*April, 1899* 139

*have gone astray. It is almost time for another. I was in hopes we would get one to day. If you said anything very interesting or important in the stray letter you will have to repeat it in your next.*

*I enjoy looking out, everything is so freshly green, so verdant. In the little book I am reading, the author speaks of April as the 'showery flowery month'. It does not deserve the latter name this year, for with the exception of the fruit trees and a few early shrubs, flowers there are not. We are having a few showers. It looks very much like rain this morning. The wind is in the east and it is quite cloudy. A man brought some nice looking strawberries to the door just now. I bought a box and am going to surprise papa with a strawberry shortcake. The man said they were home raised. They have been in the market a week or so. I wish I could give you a saucerful.*

*Mrs. Kennedy and Josey came to see me yesterday. They both looked pretty in their fresh spring costumes, the latter particularly lovely. They both asked after you. Josie said she told you before you left that she would come to see me. Kate Kerr was down also. We have secured Mr. McCan to plant the grass on Monday. Mr. Knolls did not finish up what I wanted him to do. He had grippe.*

*5:30 P.M. Before I was through washing my dinner dishes Mrs. William phoned she would come for me in a few minutes, that one of our patients had died, and we would have to see about burial clothes & c. By getting Papa to wipe the dishes, I just did get ready by the time she came. We have been driving all afternoon. Quite a cool norther is blowing, it was even cold with a wrap on. I got rather chilled, and as I have no fire in the furnace I have made one in the kitchen stove. I received a letter* from Mrs. Sutherland at noon. There is nothing of special interest in it to write you. They are keeping house.

Papa saw Charlie day before yesterday, he said the Dr. said he would not be able to wear a shoe in a long time.

It has been trying to rain all afternoon and seems to be succeeding now, quite a good shower is coming down. I have just been to the door to answer a benevolent call. They are coming pretty thick. May will soon be there and then we can say <u>next month</u>! I had intended to put in this afternoon on my history lesson. I have scarcely given it a thought this week. To morrow will be the last time I can go for several weeks on account of the meeting. The Hardware Convention meets here in Sherman two days of next week.

I saw the negative of my last <u>sitting</u> and I like it less than one of the others. I wish I had worn my black dress. I hope papa will write you something of more interest to go in this letter. Bishop Homes was here Sunday. Sports a big moustache.

Lovingly

Mamma


Dear Boy: Mama has gotten to think that I must add some to all her letters. So here goes -- I have just made a wood fire in the Furnace & we are sitting around the Dining room table, and only two registers open. One in Hall & this one. Mercury is 50 -- Yesterday heat was offensive. I got up this morning & took off my heavy Flannel & put on my summer suit at Dinner I put my Flannel back & in the morning will go back to my winter suit.

*We are a little worried about not getting any letter from you this week, but think as Mama says one has gone astray – will certainly look for one tomorrow -- and if we dont get it -- by Saturday morning I shall telephone you.*

*Nonni told me this evening we had made a big shipment to day. I was a little surprised as I had been busy & had not noticed. Beckham came in this morning bringing in some orders. Lane phoned in some. Sneed sent in some and then Harve sold two or three parties. Harve sells a good many goods. I really think to turn him loose & let him work the town trade & wait on trade from the county that come in, watch the trains as they come in and the wagons from the country merchants near Sherman, that he would beat them all. I know he would make the best profits.*

*Joe is engaged this week in advertising think he is sending out about 1500 letters or circulars in the County. I have my doubts about it paying the expense. We have a new Minograph -- fine one, cost $15.00 and he has had John busy all the week helping him. I dont believe he is going to do anything with it, he told me this morning that he would have to pay about $5.00 for seal, then about $5.00 to county clerk and some other official, perhaps Assumption Tax -- I dont recollect. It would take a good long time, situated as he is, and there being so many others* [notaries] *all over town, for him to make the money back. We dont have much swearing* [notarizing] *to do.*

*Mr. Joiner, Mr. Eubanks and myself, all went down to the Bay Mill yesterday. They are putting in New Boilers and a new Corliss Engine -- and have good many boys and some men rubbing up and oiling all the old Looms & c. They expect to get to running about middle of May. They are going to make some* money this time -- they only paid about $50,000. for the whole Plant, that cost about $175,000. -- then the new machines & to get it started up will cost about $10,000. they have either 5 or 10 years to pay the $50,000. with 10% interest -- and they expect to pay this out of their earning and declare good Dividends at same time. I had a chance to take stock in it, and wish I had. I would have done it had I been assured that the Dallas Cotton Mills would have gone into it and managed it. Chilt Andrews and Cal Eubanks went into it here. Chilt Andrews came to me and wanted me to go into it before he went to Eubanks. I believe it will make them rich, however they will probably run on Sunday during the rush of busy season and that would not suit me --

Well it is 10 oclk and bed time, as next week we are to have night service, we had better reserve our strength & c, and not sit up too late -- Mama is hunting up <u>data</u> for her tomorrow's history class dont suppose she will want to quit, but here goes. Good night. Hope you are well & studying hard, and will bear off some palms of Victory. Of course we cant and ought not expect it, ought to be satisfied & gratified to think you are doing so well -- but you know poor human nature is never satisfied. It is raining & I am afraid is going to Hail. Once more good night from Papa.

## THE TWENTY EIGHTH LETTER

From Emma and C.N. in Sherman
5 May 1899

This is another letter which perfectly captures daily life in 1899. One can almost "see" the Roberts house yard from Emma's description, and C.N. captured the essence of life at his business when he described the sales office as "so much crowded with Drummers [traveling salesmen] RR [railroad] men and other Loafers and Visitors." The employee C.N. mentioned, Sam Roberts, was no relation to the family.

The proposed trip to Atlantic City was to attend a National Hardware Convention. The venue of Atlantic City for a convention in 1899 was much like holding a business convention in Las Vegas, today.

*Friday 10 15 A.M.*
*May 5 -- 1899*

*My Dear Son;*

*We had a nice shower in the night, it is particularly nice* on our grass. It is quite cloudy this morning. We have a great deal of cloudy weather. I am afraid it is not very good on most things. My sweet peas are out near the back fence shaded on the east side by two hackberries, they are pretty thick and I noticed this morning they are turning yellow and withering in places. I have some magnificent roses in bloom this morning. The berry man has just passed. I got two boxes, one for shortcake for dinner and one to eat with cake for supper. I get the cake from Kirtley.

Charlie is still limping around, but has discarded his crutches. I expect, or rather, suppose he will be more anxious to make money than ever, when he is able to work. I have just had the yard mowed and put in nice order and everything is so fresh. I waste a good deal of time staring out, first in one direction and then in another.

Papa, Kirtley and I went to the wedding. It was a very pretty wedding, and not a bit stiff. The happy couple have gone to Cal. but for only a short time. Henry Head asked me that night about you and asked me to remember him to him to you. Last night Prof. Thompson asked after you. Many ask after you. Mrs. Lee Woods was asking me this other afternoon if I kept up with you, and if you wrote to <u>one</u> girl or many, and asked me if I had seen <u>Jim</u> I judge she had been discussing you with Jim. I am looking for a letter at noon. I want to know what you think of my pictures. They had all my palms over at the wedding and they came back, as usual, some of them, the worse for wear.

Our meeting is still in progress. Ethel told me the other night at the wedding that Edna was going to unite with the church.

Mrs. Zemanski asked for prayer yesterday. She came in

May, 1899

late to the service last night. I think she has to wait for him to leave home. Prof. Bell has been so faithful, coming twice a day.

<u>1 30</u> P.M. I have just read papa's letter. See he has given you some of the items I had intended writing. Miss Fowler asked Kirtley yesterday if I could give her some jacqueminot roses to paint. I have sent her a big bunch and some others that are handsomer. We have been having unusually pleasant weather. Not too hot to study in Texas. I think you must be dressed too warm.

Your letter came to day. What do you think of our sending you some Cape Jasamines, when they come in, for Mrs. Cameron? We could have them packed in Houston. It is time I was getting ready for church.

It is quite dark and thundering. I doubt whether I can go. Kirtley called over to know if I was going to church. I think she wants to come over.

Five O'clock. I did not go to church. Kirtley came over and has just gone. We had quite a shower, but I could have gone to church if she had not been here. I will pick my berries for supper now and get ready for church.

Lovingly Mamma

I am glad you like the picture I may never have another taken.

Dear Boy: Mama has just made me fill myself uncomfortably full of strawberry shortcake, and as usual insists upon my writing some in her letter. I feel more like taking a nap, but here goes.

Small Pox scare is affecting trade a good deal -- they get up all sorts of rumors in the country. Miss Mollie Pullen told me on the car as I came to dinner that a party reported at their store, that they had it reported in the country that were there were over 40 cases in Sherman -- when in fact I dont believe there is over 5 cases --- Mama and I were both vaccinated, on last Monday (now Friday) but no signs of taking yet.

Mike Sneed was in all day yesterday -- went to Paris [Texas] this morning you know that he was indicted in the Federal Court there more than a year ago for aiding in the shooting of a man up in the [Oklahoma] territory. I think he got into bad company and while he perhaps had nothing to do with the shooting, he was in the crowd and several were indicted, his trial comes off next week. I think he is very anxious and worried about it --

He wanted me to see and talk to Judge Bryant for him, Judge will be here Saturday.

Well Eubank is out and John has moved into Sanfords office. I am afraid Will's office is so much crowded with Drummers, R.R. men and other Loafers & Visitors that John will not be able to work as well as in my office, he told me yesterday they bothered him. Will Gough & Jim Snider did the collecting first thing this month. Sanford proposed Will in place of John. I think he will make a better collector than John, very likely we will keep him at it. Parks has been sick a week but is back in office again.

Our office work is snowed under. Ludlow is so far behind that he will never catch up. I have got to get someone to help catch up then I dont believe Ludlow will keep up. He has lost his grip. He dont try any more. I am going to talk with him in a day or two, and I expect I will stir up things -- and it may result in Ludlow's quitting -- I think Mr Parke would just as soon he would quit as not -- of course it would be much lighter on me for him to stay if he would do right, for it is no little thing to get another man and give him the experience of Mr Ludlow. Mr Parks would do his best but he would be more or less distracted by new work and in helping to break in a new man --

Lane is happy again since Will Eubanks is out. I wish Lane would put more time in on the roads -- he could if he would and sell nearly double what he does.

We have let Jim Roberts out he has opened a shop with another fellow down next to the Singer Sewing Machine office in Moore Block -- Cope & Joe worked him out, selling him most of the Bicycle shop stuff. I am mighty glad of it, for I dont think they were making any money & lots of annoyance and complaining of charges & c -- Jim ought to do well, but dont think he will ever amount to anything --

Joe is figuring up stock it will probably take him all the month, first copy then he & Sanford to price and then Joe to Extend -- a huge job -- we have a very large stock -- it will take to June 1st I am afraid to get through.

I can not determine for sometime whether I go to Atlantic City or not I may go -- I rather think they expect me to go -- & if I dont, reckon Sanford will. Well I must stop and go to the store I have lots of work ahead this afternoon -- remittances to get off.

*Good bye. It is right pleasant today -- mercury 70 now half past 1 oclk. Mama has just come in from gathering roses & wants me to take a box up & send to Miss Eva Formley -- so here goes -- good bye. From Papa ---*

[torn sheet; EER's handwriting]
*Saturday*

*It rained so hard last night that we could not go to church and hence could not mail this letter, so it will be a day late. It is still threatening rain, weeds & grass will be hard to keep down.*

## THE TWENTY NINTH LETTER

From Stanly at Princeton
5 May 1899

Stanly certainly was glad to be nearing the end of his studies when he wrote this letter. Although much less keen about studying than were his parents, Stanly had worked hard at Princeton and he had hoped to make his parents proud of him by making a spectacular finish but, as this letter explained, his final tests were not to be "counted".

*Friday -- 1 PM*

*Dear Papa & Mamma: --*

*Your letter was received on time yesterday morning. Sherman must be having a great time with the smallpox at present from all accounts.*

*I am glad that I am not there just at present not that I am afraid of the smallpox but I dont want to be vaccinated -- In some cases it isn't so very much the smaller of two evils. I certainly wouldn't be vaccinated until I was made to. They made* it compulsory in Sherman didnt they?

Every letter I write I have been intending to say something about my watch but have forgotten it. I dont know what on earth I would have done without it this year. I have only set it once since I have been here (That was when I first came) and it hasnt varied from the time which Old North keeps by as much as five <u>seconds</u> since that time. I didnt know a watch could keep such good time.

The Schedule for our exams are out. They begin May 15th & last to May 27th. I havent anything the first three days. Mine come as follows -- May 18th Prose Fiction -- May 20th Ethics -- May 22nd Bible @ 9 AM. French @ 2 PM -- May 24th Constitutional Law -- May 26th History -- May 27th Political Economy.

I have something to tell you that will probably disappoint you a little. I dont know whether I am glad or sorry.

They dont keep any record of the Senior exams for the last term. What I mean is that they dont send out any reports or do any grouping. They simply decide whether you have passed or not. If your dont pass you get a notice. If you do pass you dont get anything.

I didnt know this until just a day or two ago. You see all the honors as Salutatory & Valedictory etc are all awarded before hand and so they dont pay any attention to these exams except to see that you pass. I will pass mine all right and as that is all I have to do they wont worry me as much as if I were trying to get a fine group.

May, 1899

    *I believe I would have gotten about four first groups this time.*

    *I will get done here Saturday morning May 27th and will probably leave that afternoon for Conn. I think I will take my trunk up there with me this time. I will want more than one suit of clothes and that grip of my mine wont carry much.*

    *I think I will get me a box (soap box or something similar) and pack all my photos, pictures, books etc in it and ship it home by freight. I will pack up all my things when I leave here in May as I will only be back here two to three days at Commencement. I may be able to get everything in my trunk -- but I am not such a good packer as Papa and I am afraid I wont find the room -- for everything. I think I will take my bicycle with me too -- May has just gotten a wheel -- and learnt how to ride and she wants me to be sure and bring my wheel.*

    *I must stop now and study Constitutional Law for examination.*

    *I will certainly be glad when I can write I am through with all my exams.*

    *Goodbye with lots of love*

    *Stanly --*

## THE THIRTIETH LETTER

From Stanly at Princeton
11 May 1899

In this letter Stanly was responding to a now lost letter from his parents in which they proposed taking Stanly on "The Grand Tour" of Europe as a graduation present. With the manners born of true affection combined with a lack of innate understanding of motives, Stanly tried to express gratitude for the wish without outright mention of his lack of enthusiasm for the trip. Most probably at this point Stanly was thoroughly homesick for Sherman and his girlfriend and tremendously eager to begin in the business world. Meanwhile, Emma and C.N. probably believed Stanly had to be as disappointed as they about his lack of honors at graduation and they had thought to "ease" his entry back home with a trip that would be more talked about than would be his year at Princeton. In the end the family formed a plan that pleased all parties: the trip was delayed for a year.

Princeton N. J.
May 11th '99

Dear Folks: --

Your letter came just a few minutes ago and almost took my breath away --

I think the trip would be fine. It would be a great thing and do Papa lots of good to get off for the length of time. Of course it all depends however upon the business and how much money papa gets from it this year. I should think it would take a good deal to pay that debt, my expenses at Princeton and go abroad too. You mustn't take the trip on my account for I have had my share already. I will leave it to you all to decide.

Even if you decide not to go to Europe why cant you both come up to graduation here and then go on to Connecticut for awhile -- If you write to Mrs Hood you had better do it pretty soon as I think they expect to leave about the first of June --

I wont pack up my things to ship home by freight until about the 23rd or 24th. I believe I told you that I thought I would take my trunk to Conn with me this time.

As far as leaving to go anywhere is concerned I dont have to be here after May 27th. I know several boys that are going home and not coming back any more. You can have your diploma sent to you and dont have to be here to get it unless you want to. About my finances -- I have about $22.00 now -- I find it takes as much to graduate here and more too than it did at A.C. [Austin College] except I dont have to buy any suits. Each member of the class will be assessed about $16.00. This includes, graduating invitations, class pin, souvenir book (Nassau Herald) etc etc. The $16.00 cover all the expenses of graduation but I will have a laundry bill of $7.00 or $8.00 for the second term.

One week from today I have my first examination. One of my easiest - Prose Fiction.

It is raining here this morning -- a cold gloomy looking rain -- I guess we are having what they call "Blossom storm" here. It comes in May and generally lasts three days. I hope it wont last three days this time for day after tomorrow we have a big baseball game with Harvard.

Time doesnt fly quite so fast here a now as it did because the thought of exams and the working for them makes it go slower.

These last two weeks now will probably seem longer than the past four --

I dont know whether I will take my wheel to Conn, with me or not. It will be a good deal of trouble to have it crated to send that far and if I check it I will have the trouble of getting across N.Y. City from Jersey City to the Grand Central Station. You see I dont buy my ticket straight through from here -- I buy one ticket here to New York and then another from N. Y. to Canaan & return. If I bought my ticket straight from here it would cost me $10.50. As it is I get it for $7.00.

It is half past eleven -- very near time for lunch -- and I had no idea it was more than ten oclock. I dont have any classes to day at all. I never have but one on Thursday. Bible from Prof. Hibben and as he wound up the Bible course yesterday I havent

May, 1899

*any today.*

*I have three classes tomorrow and two Saturday and then Im done except those exams.*

*I must stop now. I will be anxious to get your next two or three letters to see what you will decide though I do not suppose you will know what you will do until the last of the month.*

*Give my love to all friends and with lots of love to yourselves I am*

*Your loving son*

*Stanly --*

## THE THIRTY FIRST LETTER

From Emma in Sherman
12 May 1899

The "case in our ward" to which Emma referred in this letter was another problem for her benevolence society in the section of town to which Emma was assigned. In the years before Federal or State assistance programs, poor families facing unusual situations such as ill health or the inability of the primary bread winner to bring home wages could hope for help only from their neighbors, their church or the community. Primarily because so many of the poorest families in Sherman at this time lived in just a few areas of town and almost all attended the same church, there was a great deal of unrelieved want until Emma and other women formed a town Benevolence Society.

So many of the problems of poverty, illness, degradation and abuse which Emma saw through her benevolent society work were caused by the effects of excessive use of alcohol that Emma became a strong proponent of mandated abstinence. Although she had enjoyed an occasional glass of wine or port in her younger years, Emma became part of the growing Temperance movement. C.N., who also saw negative effects in the business world from employees who were excessively intemperate, supported Emma in her cause and

May, 1899

the couple worked hard to sway voters to make Sherman "dry". To this day Sherman is "dry" and letters in the 1930's between Stanly and his wife, Leska, indicate that two generations of the Roberts family had much to do with making and keeping Sherman "dry".

*Sherman Friday 845 A.M.*<br>
*May 12, '99*

*Dear Sonny,*

*We have a bright morning and the birds are merry. A bright morning is rather unusual, for we are having one of those rainy spells in May, when the showers come down without trouble or warning, and the early mornings are nearly always cloudy. The berry man has just passed. I bought three boxes for a quarter. The phone has just rung. Mrs Craycroft wants to know if we can attend to a case in our ward, we will have to look after it this afternoon. Our meeting closed Wednesday night. No more accessions.*

*Charlie came yesterday to return a bowl that we took him up some berries in. He is ready to come back. I told him we might possibly go off this Summer, and if so, I would not want him until fall. He says he has an offer in the upper end of town and wants to hold that down, and would like to know as soon as possible Papa says for me to take him anyway. I hate to do that if we go, for I can save so much expense, and the place is costing us enough to keep down the weeds and grass. You know I had rich dirt put all over the yard and it is prolific of weeds, the grass also grows fast, not as fast as I would like to see it on the part that has been newly planted but I suppose as fast as I could expect. I* do not suppose I can keep Charlie waiting until I know about the business as he has been laid aside for a month and will be anxious to get to work.

Mr. Beaty said -- as we came down on the car Wed. night that if he could sell his lot on North Travis St. he wanted to buy ours South of us. I think he wants to sell his to the president of the new bank -- Mr. Blake. Mr. Robinson is trying to rent his place to the same party. The latter place has been vacant since the Wrights left.

Grace will be going home now in a short time. She will go up and spend a week with Bertha and return here to get her round trip ticket. She wants Kirtley to go with her. And Kirtley wants to do so if the way is clear. Mrs Darnall did not expect to go back to Eureka and I have an idea would like to depend on us. I am owing a good many letters, have never answered Carrie's or Bertha's and am owing Mrs. Sutherland one.

Papa has Mr. Ryan -- Frank Ryan -- in the office helping to get up the books. He would have to put someone in his place if he goes off. We do not know anything of Mr. Hardwicke's movements. We have heard several times that he intended starting in hardware business. So I would not be surprised if he did not begin in the fall. If he does in the Cunningham store there will be three hardware stores in a row. I am expecting a letter from you at noon.

Lovingly,

Mamma

## THE THIRTY SECOND LETTER

From Emma and C.N. in Sherman
2 June 1899

The gazebo on the side lawn of the C.S. Roberts Historic House Museum is so much a town symbol that the Sherman Chamber of Commerce web site uses it as a logo on their homepage and it is, of course, the symbol for the Sherman Preservation League and the Sherman Preservation League Press. Until this letter was discovered, no one remembered exactly when the family erected the gazebo on the site of their first house on the property. It is also noteworthy that the Roberts family had to have been among the first families in Sherman to replace their brick sidewalks with cement walks.

*Friday 5. P. M.*
*June 2, '99*

*Dear Sonny;*

*I am just up from quite a lolling spell. I spent quite an active morning, preserving strawberries, working in the flowers &c. So I was glad to lie down with some old Home Journals, to rest, and read.*

Mrs. Lee Woods telephoned me this afternoon that she wanted to leave Mande with me Saturday night and Sunday. She wants to go to Corsicanna. I assured her that it would be nice to have her, so I look for her to morrow afternoon. Maud was down one evening this week with her boy friend, or sweet heart from the Territory, Lucius McAdams. Perhaps you have heard her mention him. He timed his visit to take in the Commencement exercises, had the small pox permitted. Miss Susie Williams is very ill. Her recovery very doubtful. Several of her roommates are quarantined. I presume it is the most doleful time of their lives. The parents of Miss Williams are at home with another daughter who is quite ill with meningitis. How great their trouble.

There are several new cases of small pox, but in the same families where it has been. Two Dodson brothers and a Mrs. Cravens who nursed her child. Kirtley is getting ready to go off with Grace, they may go next week and possibly may wait until the first of July to get the benefit of the Endeavor rates. Mrs. Noble is going to take a cottage up on lake Erie for the Summer, so they expect to have a fine time.

Margie came over and sat with me a while one afternoon. She and Kirtley have received your invitations. I never do see Jim. Finette is looking quit well. I saw her in a store and was very much surprised. I have heard others express surprise at how well she is looking. Papa sent you a small check yesterday and will send another to Princeton. I imagine this year has come up to all of your anticipations and that you would not willingly lose it from your experience.

I am glad you took your wheel. You and May will have a

June, 1899

good time riding together. We are talking of having the cement walks laid and the 'pagoda' -- summer house --- made. Prof. Rosebro left yesterday. He says his father is an alumnus of Princeton. He -- the father -- will attend the Commencement. Prof. Rosebro says he will tell him to look you up. We continue to have high dry winds. Prof. Morrison will be here for several days I think. I have run out of something to say and must go and put my preserves in the jars. With much love to all.

Lovingly,

Mamma


Dear Boy

I did expect to write you a little in mama's letter but Kirtley & Miss Darnall are down on Porch & so I cant this time -- I have about 150 statements to send off but dont mean I will get them off to night -- this is the first lot "North & East Route" -- will have them all tomorrow. Capt Ryan is still helping in the office -- he is very quick. Well good night for this time

Love to all

From

Papa

## THE THIRTY THIRD LETTER

From Emma and C.N. in Sherman
12 June 1899

    As this letter shows, there were always small dramas to be played out which of course seemed like great events to the principles. The "crest fallen set" at Princeton mentioned here were so on account of the final baseball game, while meantime back in Sherman Kirtley Darnall, a shadowy figure, faded more completely into the mists of time. Perhaps news of Stanly's girlfriend had been told to her for just before Stanly was to return home, she quietly determined to leave town. Recollections of her lingered in the family for years, for Emma always kept a picture of Kirtley in her room. It became such a family joke among Leska's and Stanly's children that Kirtley was the girl Stanly was "supposed" to marry that their youngest son, Royston, visited Kirtley's sister, Irene, in California when she was an elderly woman.

June, 1899                                                              163

Monday 1 30 P.M.<br/>June 12, 1899

Dear Sonny,

It is very pleasant and breezy. At this hottest part of the day the thermometer registers nearly 86. We received your note written from Conn. this morning. It is hard for us to realize that you are having such intense weather. If it continues hot there and so pleasant here, it will be a nice change for you to come home.

By this time you are aware that Cope will attend the H.C. [Hardware Convention] and that you can join him in a day or two. I think while Cope is putting in his week in N.Y. it would nice for you to visit Washington. You will never have as good a chance to do it again, perhaps you could get Cope to go too, though that is quite doubtful. And then if you could visit Boston it would be a great thing. It is very different from any other City. But we want you to do just as you please.

We saw in the Sunday paper that Princeton was beaten, no hurrahs, no bon fires, on Saturday night but a crest fallen set, telling how it was done. I am sorry Princeton was beaten. After her good success all the year it was too bad to have to wind up with two defeats.

I am sorry you will not be back in time to see Kirtley for she does not expect to come back. I did not know this until Saturday night. Mrs. Darnall expects to teach here one more year. She is going to rent her house and keep Irenes room. She has recently papered and fixed it up, repapered the parlor also. Kirtley says there is no outlook here for her profession -- Domestic Science

-- She is going to try for a position north. When she is established she wants Mrs. Darnall to come. Her going is very much like Irene's. I can hardly realize it and am so sorry about it. She does not want anything said about it. I will not try to write to you again, but you must keep us posted as to your whereabouts.

Papa has just telephoned me that we will have to take two trustees to morrow.

I am looking for Mrs. Williams to come for me to go on a benevolent case. I have a crate of blackberries to prepare for preserving in the morning. I will stop now perhaps papa can write a word.

Lovingly,

Mamma


P.S. Give our kind regard to Dr. Taylor


Nothing to write to night. Keenes gets off for a <u>two week</u> to Town to morrow morning. Parky is off for some time as a rest but in town. Papa

**CONCLUSION**

With this letter the series concludes as gently and serenely as it began. No major news had overtly controlled the tone of the year's letters but they were not entirely without incident; the Spanish American War and the dreadful smallpox epidemic had both had mention. Names of the famous Frances Folsom Cleveland and the soon to be very famous Woodrow Wilson had graced the pages in the course of the correspondence. News of train travel and bicycles and the changing fashions in mens nightwear set the letters in their time period, while stories of studying and of gardening and of business make the letters transcend the era in which they were written.

All too often the stuff of daily life is not what makes it into the history textbooks but it is that very lack of the extraordinary which makes these letters so appealing. Emma's garden, CN's business and Stanly's bicycling seem so vivid because they have not been drowned out by big historical dramas. Thanks to thirty-three brittle letters, three people who lived one hundred years ago have come to seem like people we know. In their affection for each other and their desire to share the events of their lives during a year apart they also have taught us, today, about a world so like and yet so different from our own.

Perhaps the greatest aspect of these letters is the sincerity and goodness which comprised the characters of all three writers. None were without their faults but all were earnest in their desire to live as their faith dictated. It was not long after this collection of letters was written that Emma presented a Christmas present to her son which was inscribed with the quote that was a governing principle for all the Roberts family: "'Every man should have a fine-sized cemetery in which to bury the faults of his friends' To the dearest of sons".

And so we leave the family. It is hard to believe that most of us did not really ever meet them but only visited them through their letters.